Trip to Russia
1930

Isaac Stanley Walker's
Trip to Russia 1930

Compiled & edited by
William A. Walker, Jr. & Joan Walker Miskell

𝔴𝔪
WalkerMiskell Publishing

WM

WalkerMiskell Publishing
Beacon, New York

ISBN 978-1-365-40388-0

First Paperback Printing: February 2017

Contact: wwalker7395@yahoo.com or jwmiskell@gmail.com

Table of Contents

Preface

The Five Year Plans of the Soviet Union created by General Secretary Joseph Stalin were a series of nationalized plans for the Union's economic development. The first five year plan was implemented between 1928 and 1932. It focused on rapid industrialization and the collectivization of agriculture. During this period workers constructed dams, roads, railways and canals, which all helped to expand industry and manufacturing.

Starting in the1920's, thousands of foreign workers came to the Soviet Union to work on these projects, initially many laborers, however in the 1930's an increasing number of technical specialists and skilled workers arrived. It was in this period, in May 1930, that Isaac Stanley Walker, a civil engineer from Philadelphia was commissioned by the T. A. Gillespie Company of New York City, to visit Moscow, U.S.S.R. to study the water and sewer facilities of the city and report findings and recommendations on his return. He was accompanied by Mr. John F. Skinner, a Consulting Engineer from Rochester, New York.

Isaac Walker kept a daily diary of his professional and personal activities. The diary, which includes the daily notations made during his trip to Russia, was published in the book *Over the Spillway*, December 2015. *Trip to Russia 1930* serves as an addendum to that publication, containing previously unpublished material relative to his trip. The Russia trip diary entries are republished here.

In his diary Isaac Walker wrote of preparing and submitting a report to the Gillespie Company in August 1930 with his findings and recommendations. There was no copy of that report among his papers, however a hand written draft of the report was discovered in recent years. It was transcribed and is now presented in this book for the first time.

On October 23, 1930, he delivered an address "The Water and Sewerage Works of Moscow, U.S.S.R." to the annual meeting of the Pennsylvania Water Works Association in Atlantic City, New Jersey. His copy of that address is included in this book, along with a previously unpublished transcript of an informal discussion with the Atlantic City audience. In the May 1931 Journal of the American Water Works Association, Volume 23, Number 5, his address was published as a Journal article.

A skilled photographer, Isaac Walker documented his trip with photographs which he preserved in a personal album. It is presented in its entirety here, as the pictures correspond to notations in both the diary and his discussions in the report.

Diary Entries

to Russia

1930

In May 1930, Isaac Stanley Walker and Mr. John F. Skinner, Consulting Engineer of Rochester, New York, were commissioned by the T.A. Gillespie Company of New York, to visit Moscow, U.S.S.R. to study existing sites in accordance with a program arranged by the Chief Engineer. Afterward, they visited several of the proposed sites for future water supply. They participated in numerous conferences with Russian engineers and officials. Upon return to Philadelphia, Isaac S. Walker presented the T.A. Gillespie Company a detailed report of their findings, including conclusions and recommendations.

MAY

Notes - Trip to Russia

Tuesday, 20 Left Frankford for New York by auto at 10:40 a.m. Bill drove. In party... Lil, Ruth, Helen, Bill, Mary & myself. Arrived Jersey City about 1 p.m. New concrete road to N.Y. reduces running time a lot. Lunch in Jersey City. About 2:10 called at #7 Dey St., NYC & obtained $100 in travelers checks of American Express Co. #N923468-923472 for $20 each, and P704249-704266 for $50 each. Affiliated with Chase National Bank. In case of loss, give immediate notice by telegraph to nearest American Express office.

Saw Mr. Gillespie & Mr. Jones. Took Lil to office to meet them. Drove to pier, Bush Terminal, Pier 4, 58th St., Brooklyn and left trunk (wardrobe) and suitcase. Drove to Coney Island and spent some time there. Drove to Kings Highway to see our old home and show Ruth where she was born. Drove through Prospect Park. Supper in tea room near Fort Hamilton. Back to Pier 4, and boarded boat, S.S. Bremen, about 7:30. After getting settled in stateroom, toured the boat which is the best work in modern floating hotels - everything done with the utmost in luxurious accommodations. Our stateroom, #257 outside room, is as large as a modern hotel room. Has 2 beds, bath, shower, with our bed fitted with a drop Pullman berth, so that the room will accommodate 3 persons. Bath, gray tiled halfway up, with hot and cold, fresh and salt water. Note that call buttons for steward or stewardess are alongside of tub. Also, each toilet room has a half door panel from which access may be had from the outside hall, in case of need! An example of German thoroughness.

The boat is a marvel. 940 feet long, 101 feet wide, 51,600 tons displacement. Mary, Grace, Hannah, George, Helen, Harry Getty & Stan Piland drove over from Phila. to see me off. They all left about 9:30 p.m., when I had to say goodbye to all, and to Lil, Bill, Ruth & Helen for 3 months or more. Before they left, a steamer basket with fruit, nuts & candy arrived for Mr. Skinner & myself from Mr. T.H. Gillespie wishing us bon voyage. It was mighty nice of him. Mr. Aldon Smith, V.P., Seabrook Engineering Corp. called about 9:45, and Mr. Seaver Jones, V.P., T.A. Gillespie Co. and an in-law of Mr. Thos. Gillespie, a few minutes later. Mr. Skinner (John F.) arrived about 10 p.m. Mr. Skinner, deputy city engineer of Rochester, is my co-partner in this investigation, and will be my companion for the next 3 months. He is 63 years old, but hardly looks over 40. I met him at Rochester about 1917. Mr. Smith left a number of papers with me - two sealed letters to Mr. Seabrook, a letter to be mailed at Cherbourg, a report for Mr. Seabrook, also a package of pamphlets on Seabrook Farms in N.J.

After chatting & touring the boat again, they left about 11:30 p.m., the time for visitors to go ashore. There were hundreds of visitors. Mr. Skinner & I retired about 12:30 a.m. after unpacking. My trunk was not brought into the stateroom until about 12 o'clock, and I was beginning to get somewhat concerned about the delay. The beds are very comfortable - linen sheets. The ship left the dock about 2:30 a.m. daylight time.

Wednesday, 21 Arose about 8:30 daylight time. Breakfast. At our table was Mr. Donner of Phila. Found him to be a brother of Frank Donner, formerly President of our Greencastle Water Co. - in steel business. Several steamer chairs on the Sonnen Deck (sun deck), and spent several hours in a.m. & p.m. Weather clear, sky blue - no clouds, quite warm in sun, but cool in shade. Slept for a while in chair. No motion to boat. Played deck games with Skinner. Spent several hours in ballroom in eve. Retired 12 o'clock.

Thursday, 22 Cloudy - heavy sea. The boat rolled quite heavily from 3 a.m. until late in afternoon. Heavy wind from stern. All chairs fastened to floor. Rails on all tables in dining room. All open decks wet from spray. Made further inspection of boat. Saw swimming pool - beautifully arranged. Played deck games - ping pong & deck pool with Mr. Skinner. For lunch, Mr. ...., who is at our table, and who won the pool last night, treated to wine. The pool is auctioned off every eve - 20 numbers on the day's run. For run ending this noon, the numbers were 610 to 629. Each number is auctioned and seem to bring prizes from $50 to $125 or thereabout. Then the low and high choice of the field is auctioned. High field brought $320. Mr. Donner bid $120 for low. Mr. .... won with $614, which was the day's run. Pool had over $1400 in it. Boat quieted down in afternoon. Played table tennis and went to movies. Picture called *The White Devil*... German picture - not very interesting. Dressed for dinner. Dinner at 7:45. Caviar, pompano & lobster. Rhine wine - 1926. Sat in lounge with Mr. Skinner, and Mr. & Mrs. Rodenbeck from Rochester - friends of Mr. Skinner. Sat in bar room for auction of boat speed chances. Had several steins of beer with Mr. & Mrs. Rodenback. Retired about 11:30.

Friday, 23 Beautiful day. Clear & warm. Arose about 7:30 a.m. Swam in pool before lunch. Concluded dinner about 9 p.m. Watched dancing in ballroom, and pool auctioning in smoking room. Run for day, up to noon - 631 nautical miles. Lord Tennyson, one of the passengers, is heavy gambler on the pools. Is a heavy set young man, apparently about 30 years old. Appears to be a great sport. Retired about 11:30.

ISW and J.F. Skinner on S.S. Bremen
May 23

Saturday, 24 Cloudy, but no heavy sea - some fog. Mr. Skinner said foghorn was blowing during night. I didn't hear it. Got prints of films I took in Coney Island from photographer, also copy of shots he took on deck at the time, showing Mr. Skinner & myself. Secured railroad ticket from Bremen to Berlin - $14.70. Checked trunk through to Moscow - $19.55. Cost a lot for baggage.

Chatted for an hour with Mr. Donner in the a.m. Sat in ballroom for an hour in afternoon, watching horse races. Won 4:1 on #6 in first race. Lost next 3 - came out even. Swim in pool at 4 o'clock. Moving pictures at 5 p.m. Picture was *Disraeli* and was excellent. In ballroom in eve until 10:30. Danced once with Mrs. Rodenback, friend of Skinner. Had coffee & Benedictine with Mr. Hetzer and several steins later in smoking room. Retired 12:30 or 1:30 on advanced time. Clocks are set ahead 1 hour every day.

Passenger Deck

Deck Sports

Sunday, 25 Cloudy. Mean day in a.m. Arose about 7:45, and out on the deck at 8:20, to see the airplane catapulted from ship at 8:30. Took a snapshot. Two-passenger plane - went off fine. Will carry mail to Cherbourg in advance of ship. We are due at Cherbourg tomorrow morning. Very quiet day on boat. Read. Ballroom & smoking room in eve.

Airplane on catapult ready for takeoff – May 25

Takeoff – May 25

Monday, 26 Arrived Cherbourg about 7:30 a.m. Mr. Donner left here for Paris. Two tenders took off passengers, and luggage and mail. The weather continued cloudy and chilly. Ocean calm in channel. Not able to see much of French shore. Arrived at Southampton in afternoon. Weather a little brighter. Appears to be a fine harbor. English shore line quite hilly. Passengers and luggage taken off in tenders. Took several pictures of tenders leaving. Band played as they left. Tender circled ship and then steamed for harbor, after which we started off on the last lap for Bremen, due to arrive about 11 a.m. tomorrow.

Shortly after leaving Southampton, fog became very heavy, and fog horn blowing. Many times boat stopped and backed water. About 2 years ago, the Bremen sunk another boat in a fog. Fog continued all night, and progress very slow. Many ship officers on deck. Spent some time on deck with Skinner & Hetzer watching fog. Champagne for dinner in eve. Spent an hour or more in lounge over coffee and cordials. Wonderful meals on boat. Packed trunk in afternoon.

Tuesday, 27 Arose 7:30. Still cloudy and cool, but fog lifted, and making good speed. We are about five hours late, and will not reach Bremerhaven until about 4 o'clock. Completed packing in a.m. Weather cleared after lunch In bow of boat going up North Sea approaching Bremerhaven. Chatted with _____ formerly of Wilkes-Barre, and associated with Fowler, Dick and Walker. He knows Malcolm Barnside.

Arrived Bremerhaven about 4:30 p.m. Inspection of passports in lounge by Custom officials. Passed off boat and gave up landing ticket. Wonderful system. All small baggage, suitcases taken off to examining platform by conveyors. Baggage arranged alphabetically. Picked out case in 'W's, and laid it on platform to be examined. Examination not very thorough. No questions asked. Mr. Hetzer accompanied us to the train which left at 5:37 or 17:37 by the station clock. I had seat 24 in compartment 9, first class. There are 7 compartments to a car; each can accommodate 6 persons, but generally they only sell 4. The first class cars are very luxurious, equal to our finest Pullmans. Large windows, about 4' wide. Ventilators, glass (2) windows; & door opening on corridor with large window opposite our corridor so you can see out on both sides of train. If privacy is desired, pull down curtains. Ash trays, hinged writing table, pillows, luggage rack, coat & hat rack, electric chandelier, etc... pictures & mirrors.

Places in dining car are assigned by ticket. We elected to eat at the third table at 8 o'clock, table seat 384. The dining car is in 2 divisions. Kitchen at end. Each division to hold 24 seats. Fixed seats facing tables. 4 tables seating 4, and 4 seating 2 in each division. Meal is table d'hote, cost 3.30 marks - about 82 cents. Two waiters serve each division. Had soup, omelet with sausages, roast veal, lettuce, cheese & crackers. No dessert. No water. Had coffee - 40 pfennigs extra, and pint of Bordeaux - cost 2.90 marks or 70 cents. Total bill (for 2) was 10.30, with 10% or 1.03 added for tip, or Bedienung - or 11.33 marks or $2.72. The food was very good. No butter service until the cheese course at end of meal. Almost everyone drank beer or wine. The head waiter collects at end... comes around with a tray piled with silver & copper marks & pfennings. There is a toilet at each end of the compartment car. Each are used both by men & women. Only 1 person - 1 seat. No urinal. Handle to raise seat. Flushes when seat is lowered.

The country was quite interesting. Flat. Between Bremerhaven and Bremen low green pasture lands, with ditches, protected by dykes. Many herds of cows. Milkmaids milking in fields - buckets on poles. A few goats. Interesting small farm houses. Many brick, with thatched roofs. Several large wind mills. In small towns, or near by, thousands of small truck gardens. Funny red & white gates at rail crossings. Policemen at station at Bremen in green suits, black shiny leather hats. Conductors in brilliant blue suits. Some attendants, probably porters, in black pants, blue coats and red hats. Gravel railbed near Bremerhaven. White insulators on telegraph poles.

A very interesting German gentleman shared our compartment. He spoke English, also Russian, Persian, etc. Traveled around world and lived in Persia for long period. Evidently well-to-do, in textile business. Lives in suburb of Berlin. Got off train about midnight at Friedrichstrasse Bahnhof station... lower the wide window in compartment and call porters who wait along platform. Pass valises, etc. out window. He loads on small flat truck. Trucks go down elevator, and he lines up on sidewalk and waiting taxis. We went to Hotel Adlon on Unter den Linden. Said to be about best hotel in Berlin. Secured a fine room for 38 marks per day for 2, including 10% tip. Large room. Twin beds - beautifully furnished. Excellent service. Large bathroom. Tub long enough to stretch out.

Wednesday, 28 Arose about 8 a.m. Breakfast in Adlon. Continental breakfast of fruit, toast & rolls, marmalade & coffee, tea or chocolate. marks. Left about 9:30 to look up Mr. Luberski, or Dorothea Stresse. He is Seabrook's Berlin representative. Had great difficulty in finding him. Finally located him, and found him to be a very affable Russian gentleman, about my age... an engineer. Lives in U.S. He took us to Russian embassy and started us on way of getting passports. There we met a Mr. Bessey, a young engineer on way to Moscow, also to do some work for Seabrook on river harbor work. A young man from the Hamburg American line gave us considerable assistance. We finally received the passports about 12:30. The Hamburg American man took them to the Polish Consul's office and secured the visas to go through Poland, but did not return until 3 o'clock.

Took a ride for an hour about town with Skinner... had some lunch and beer at the Kroll, a fine large beer garden. Returned to Adlon about 4:15 and met Mr. Luberski. Had some tea & beer, and Skinner bought some coffee & cigars to take to Moscow. Met Bessey at hotel, and about 8:15 went to Winter Garden. It's a very large theater, with immense stage. Smoke in theater. At pause, or intermission, people adjourn to bars for beer, eats and coffee. Saw a rather mediocre vaudeville show. After show went to Kempenski Vaterland - a remarkable place in huge building, with many restaurants and eating rooms, furnished in accord with customs of different nations. First saw a very realistic representation of a storm on the Rhine Valley - sehr gut. Then at about 11 o'clock, went to dance or ballroom. Waiter saw we were strangers, and escorted us to a ringside table by the dance floor. We ordered dinner and had a very nice meal with wine. The cabaret lasted until 1 a.m., a 2 hour show. Had about 20 or 25 girls and an excellent show. Cost 1 mark to get in building, and 1 mark added cover charge for cabaret. Had filet mignon, potatoes, strawberries & cream and small bottle Rhine wine. Total cost for 3, including cover charge 19 marks. In N.Y. or Phila. would cost 25 or 30 dollars. Back to hotel about 1:30.

Thursday, 29 Beautiful clear day. Arose 9 a.m. Breakfast at Adlon. Wrote letter to Lil and post cards to all the children, and Mary, Jule, & Lillie. Bessey came to hotel about 12 o'clock. Left about 1:30 with him and hired a Buick car and guide and drove to Potsdam. Beautiful drive, about 25 miles; out Bismark Strasse & Wilhelm Strasse to Potsdam Blvd, a toll speedway for automobiles which formerly the Emperor's finest rode to his castle in Potsdam. Passed through beautiful parks & homes. Through Kastel-Wannsee, a popular park and resort with beautiful lake for bathing, boating, fishing, etc. Saw in distance thousands of bathers. Yacht regatta, canoes, launches, etc. Nearer Potsdam passed another fine lake. Potsdam old city of 60,000. Beautiful old homes, many wealthy retired Germans live there. The first thing we saw was the old church (Lutheran). Cost 1/2 mark to enter. It is the tomb of Fredrich the Great and his father, Fredrich 1st. Beautiful church... altar, pulpit, pews for congregation at each end. Royal chairs for Emperor opposite pulpit. Built by Fredrich 1st. Sanssouci (without a care) built by Fredrich 1st - wonderful park and grounds, old mill nearby. New schloss or castle built by Fredrich the Great. Went all through with guide. Have to put felt sandals over shoes. Wonderful rooms, pictures by old artists. Crystal room stones from all over world. Home of Kaiser Wilhelm. Saw tomb of Kaiser who died 6 or 7 years ago in Holland. He left request in will to be buried near his rose garden where different part of life was spent with his children. Walked through grounds - beautiful terraces.

Roy F. Bessey & German Guide   *ISW & German Guide*
Stop enroute to Potsdam sampling a Pilsner, Muenchner & Wurzenburger

Left about 3:15 and back to Adlon at 4:30. Mr. Luberski called but left before we returned. Packed bag & Skinner's trunk. Got to railroad station about 5:50. Train was 20 minutes late. Left Friedrichstrasse Bahnhof at 6:10 p.m. - on way to Moscow. Had compartment first class. Unable to get sleeper. Supper on train - fair. Had some difficulty making waiter understand. During meal met a man & wife, Mr. & Mrs. Patton. He is a sanitary engineer staying in Russia for 2 years for Austin Co., about 200 miles from Moscow. Had to stay up until after 11 p.m. for Customs examination at Polish border. At border, soldiers board train & collect passports. Very strict. Many soldiers at station. All trunks taken off and carted in station to examining platform. They examined suitcases on train. Did not look at boxes. Weighed Skinner's trunk and brought it back without opening. Country through Germany interesting. No mountains - flat - beautiful forests of pines - well taken care of. Double seats, crosswise of train in compartment. A Pole came in our compartment at the Polish border and remained in compartment until we arrived at Posen. I slept on upper berth in clothes & overcoat & dressing gown. No bed clothes. Slept pretty well.

Friday, May 30 On train all day. Breakfast about 8 a.m. Poland landscape not very interesting. Stopped at Warsaw for 15 or 20 minutes. Polish name Varshava. Several apparently high class Polish girls at station to see mother off train. Dressed well, and about same as American girls. A number of priests at station. Arrived at Stolpce, last station in Poland about 4 p.m. More soldiers & Customs examinations. There about 45 mins. Arrived Niejerola,

Russian border, about 5:20 p.m. Communist soldiers boarded train and collected passports. I got acquainted on the train with a Polish man named Hoski who had lived in U.S. for past 20 years, and graduated in M.E. from Michigan University. He spoke Polish and Russian fluently and helped us in our Customs negotiations. Examination of our luggage was perfunctory. Station built of logs - quite large. Strange people - rough dress. Many wear hair close cropped. Porters are in greasy dirty looking garb. Everything crude. Purchased first class sleeper accommodations to Moscow. Cost 19.5 rubles or about $10. Changed a $20 travelers check and obtained $38.64 rubles. Skinner tried to change two $50 checks and the Russian gentleman would not accept them - said his signature was not the same. It pays to have a clear, bold signature under these circumstances. Took a picture from train window at border. Soviets here erected a steel arch over the tracks on the boundary line, which reads in Russian hieroglyphics "Communism erases all boundary lines.

J.F. Skinner & A.H. Hoski
Brief stop in Warsaw

Stolpce Train Station
Last station in Poland

Off for Moscow again about 7 o'clock. Time advances 1 hour here. We are now 6 hours ahead of Phila. daylight saving time, or 7 hours ahead of standard time. Had lunch on train with Mr. & Mrs. Potter, and supper with Mr. Hoski. Prices on Russian train absurd. A tureen of fish soup cost 1.75 rubles, dinner cost about 6 rubles with a bottle of beer & cordial. Had berth made up about 10 o'clock. Russian sleeping cars are very elaborate in appearance. Compartment about 7'x7'+/-. Accommodations elaborate but not very comfortable. Beds good. Ventilator in.......... Very dusty, sand ballast after leaving Poland. Railbed rough, cars rock badly. No clothes hangers, no soap, no towels, no toilet paper or hot water. Drinking water boiled, in .... in wash compartment. Not very clean. Slept well until 3:30, then awake several hours. They turn off electricity at night about 2 a.m. or so, not able to read. Stays light until 9:30 or thereabout. Dawn about 3 a.m.

Saturday, 31 Arose about 7. Porter brought tea and cakes in room. Tea very good - served in glasses. Drank in bed. Breakfast at 7:30. Had cup of chocolate and package of biscuits. Chocolate -6 rubles or about 32 cents a cup. Package of crackers - 1 ruble - 2 cents. Absurd prices.

Arrived in Moscow about 9:30 a.m. Mr. George Perelatrius met us at train. Drove in taxi to Hotel Savoy. General condition difficult of description — general amount of dilapidation, buildings in terrible shape. People dressed poorly. Old style for conveyances for everyone. Ford taxis all owned by government. Government runs everything. Hotel once very good... now fair, but service far different from Berlin & home. Went to Seabrook office & met Mr. Seabrook and Mr. Perelatrius, Sr., his Russian contact man. Very fine gentleman, U.S. citizen. They took us to see the mayor but he was out. Then saw the Commissar - Communist in charge of the Department of Water and Canalization (Sewage). Dressed in Russian garb, shaved head, short, etc. Met Mr. Gooshine, engineer in charge of water; and Mr. Zuyagunion, engineer in charge of sanitary sewers and sewage disposal. They don't speak English. Mr. Perelatrius acted as interpreter. Discussed program, and secured some general information. Sewage is called canalization.

Lunch at Savoy - excellent. Chicken cutlet. To Seabrook's office after lunch, then to Savoy to meet Mr. Bessey who arrived by airplane from Berlin about 2:30 p.m. Chatted in hotel. Dinner at 8 p.m. with Mr. Seabrook,

Perelatrius, Sr., Skinner, Bessey and Mr. Milligan. Latter is a C.P.A. for Seabrook, a brother of Bob Milligan, former president of N.Y.C.J. Filtration Co. The hotels are all crowded, and we had to take a room at the Europa Hotel. Not very satisfactory. To hotel room about 9 p.m. and wrote up notes, etc. A further study of the city and the life and habits of this people under this great experiment will be of interest. The population is in the neighborhood of 2,600,000, and increasing at the rate of about 1/2 million a year. Their facilities are inadequate for so many. Saw hundreds of people in lines in streets to get food, supplies, etc. from government stores. It would appear that many hours of their time is spent in waiting in lines. A la carte meals at restaurants are extremely high in price. Food at other than good hotels is poor and filthy. Cigarettes at present can't be bought. Coffee is very dear in restaurants. Cocoa is fair. Tea good. Toilet paper and writing paper scarce. Almost everything high in price. Brandy is cheap - also vodka. Both good. Brandy 5 rubles a bottle. Money inflated, fixed by government at rate of 1.94 or. Fictitious value. Wages of workers fixed by government. Many earn only 50 or 60 rubles a month. With prices for everything at such high rates, impossible to understand how existence is possible.

JUNE

Sunday, 1 Arose about 7:30. Clear in early a.m. Had difficulty in getting breakfast. Service terrible. Finally got come chocolate and a couple of eggs. To office at 9. Friday (Russian man of all work) took Skinner & me to Customs station for trunks. Examined. Held up for further exam of technical books. Back to office at 10:15. The Commissar of the Water & Canalization Trust sent a young man interpreter, and we went to Sewage office. Auto was provided. Visited sewage plants with assistant engineer in charge, Mr. Alifato, and Professor Stroganov (chemist and bacteriologist). Both very fine and capable gentlemen. Saw sewage pumping station and disposal fields at Luberski. Very extensive sand filters. Lunch about 1 p.m. at Workers Club. Also tea about 6. Entertained us very nicely - good hosts. Weather strange... very cold, snow flurries which lasted 10-15 minutes. Wind storm blew sand at sewage fields. Fields about 12-15 miles from city. Very interesting drive. Horses ahead of autos. Peasant houses - decorated. Community Club for Soviet workers. Visited plant hospital - white aprons to enter. Back at hotel at 2:30. Light lunch at Savoy with Bessey & Mr. Milligan. To Europa at 10:30... had bath & enjoyed for short time. No baths in rooms - 1 bathroom to each floor. Poor facilities. No gas or central plant for hot water. Heat water in wood-fired boiler in bathroom. Only provided me with one very thin towel - had run out of bath towels. Found our trunks in room, but Friday did not return trunk key, and I could not open it.

Main Sewage Pumping Station

Starting 2nd from left: Serge (interpreter),
Prof. S.N. Stroganov & L.A Alifato

Monday 2 Arose 7:30. Breakfast in room which is general custom. Prices absurd. Cup of cocoa 80 cents or 1 ruble. Omelet 75 cents. Costs 3 rubles for cup cocoa, omelet, brown bread, butter. Our engineer escorts of yesterday called at our hotel together with our young interpreter, Serge, and we left in the 14 year old auto for Lublinow plant. Extensive sewage fields, and lagoon with outfield into Moscow River. River very beautiful. Hilly at site of fields - about 100 yards wide. Saw interesting experimental plant. Had lunch about 2:30 at Workers Club. Very good lunch. Much tea and hard boiled eggs. Next went to Kashnjov plant... modern up to date activated sludge plant. Present capacity 3 mgd, increasing to 9 mgd. Optimal to have capacity of 45 mgd. Have to reconstruct my ideas of Russian Engineers. Professor Stroganow is a thorough master of technique of sewage disposal. Had nice lunch and tea in Workers Club. Left plant 7:30 and returned to hotel. Dinner at Savoy - ordered filet mignon for 4 rubles, but the fellow did not understand, and we didn't get it. A bowl of soup, a few vegetables and cup of chocolate cost about 6 rubles. Called on Bessey in his room, and chatted until 11 p.m. Had diarrhea from some of the food or water.

Tuesday, 3 Arose 7:30. Breakfast in room. Cost about $1.75 for a cup of chocolate, omelet and black bread. No fruits. Went to office about 9. Serge, our young interpreter called for us about 9:30, and we went to office of the Water & Canalization Trust. Spent day until 4 p.m. reviewing data on sewage plants, and translating Professor Stroganow's written description of their new Kashnjow activated sludge plant. To hotel room - wrote letter home. Dinner with Skinner, Bessey & Milligan. Took walk around town and saw a Russian show. Cost 1.18 rubles. Appeared to be propaganda, depicting overthrow of Capitalism and ultimate victory of Communism. Some of characters appear to be Unchours. Retired about 11.

Wednesday 4 Arose 7:30. Breakfast in room. Cocoa & omelet. To Seabrook's office at 9. To Trust office at 10, and left with asst. chief engineer of Water Works to visit Rublevsky pumping station & filter plant. Have a wonderfully fine plant. Double filtration similar to Phila. Fine laboratories - well operated. Now building the last extension of........ In many ways plant is operated more carefully than some of our works at home. Weather cloudy and cold. Dinner at 6:30 at Savoy. Had orchestra tonight. Many Americans here. One man & wife with 4 children. Secured tickets for Russian opera house, built in 1853 after the fire - 6 tiers of boxes, Czar's box in center of first tier. Ballet *Raymonda*, a revival of an old work. Very beautiful. About 100 on stage... about 70 in orchestra. Finest music - perfectly trained cast. To hotel about 10:40.

Thursday, 5 Up 7:30... stopped at Seabrook office at 8:55 and left with Serge for Commissar's office. Left with chief engineer Gooshine in old car for Mitrichensky station and Oldenbergovsky pumping station. Passed Krestovsky Towers on way out. Massive brick structures. Groundwater system. Returned about 4. Chatted after supper until 9:30. To room - wrote a few postcards and retired.

Friday, 6 Breakfast in room. To water works office at 9 a.m. Left about 9:45 in old Mercedes touring car to inspect Variobesky distributing reservoir - covered. Very nice piece of work. From there drove to Rublevsky to see new dam across Moscow River, now under construction. Are working on large rubber dam - rubber lift dam. Returned to water office at 1:30, lunch in office, then spent afternoon until 5 reviewing general water scheme using interpreter Serge. After supper in Savoy took walk in White City with Bessey & Skinner. Better section - asphalt streets. To Europa about 9:30. Wrote some postcards and retired.

On trip to Upper Moscow River in 14 year old Mercedes
From left: Serge, ISW & Commissar Kanyguine (left of car)

Inlet and gate chambers at the Variobesky Reservoir

Saturday, 7 Impossible breakfast in room. Eggs raw. Dumbest waiters ever. Stopped at office - no mail. To water office at 9 a.m., and left with engineer Vodkovski in charge of dams for site of Estra reservoir. Drove out about 20 miles. Viewed site from both sides of stream. Propose an earth dam about 17 meters high above present level - 2 meters freeboard. No core wall. Length 450 to 480 meters, storage about 110 mil. cubic meters. Will back up water about 25 km. Took drive to site. Interesting drive. Took some photos of peasant homes. All horses in outlying districts afraid of autos. Several turned off road across dark gutters. One threw old woman out on head. Dam site near town of Voskresensk. Went thru historic old Jerusalem church, built in 1656 by patriarch Nihon — old paintings, old ceramics of 16th century - blue & white & gold. Had lunch in house in village - very crude. No conveniences, bare floors, no running water. Engineer who escorted us brought the lunch. Tea in Russian samovar. Went back to hotel about 6:30. Dinner party at the Savoy with about 15 of Seabrook's men and Mr. Seabrook. Others - Messrs. Hitchcock, Nash, Shattuck, Smith, Bessey, Milligan, Perelatrius Sr. & Jr., Skinner. Very fine dinner. Have better impression of Russian cooking. Vodka, cognac, wine. In room after dinner with men until 11. Had run-in with Skinner - impossible.

Sunday, 8 No Sundays in Moscow. Terrible breakfast... two semi raw eggs, stale bread, weak coffee like medicine. Serge came about 9 a.m. & we translated part of report on water system. Lunch at Savoy. To water office from 1 to 4 p.m. reviewing Oka Project. Dinner with Bessey & Skinner. Bessey left for Leningrad for a few days. Wrote letter to Mr. Gillespie re situation. Stomach upset from the food - up several times in night.

Monday, 9 Arose 8:30. Only glass cocoa for breakfast. Left about 9:45 in old open car for Oka River - 70 mile drive. Arrived all right about 12:15. Very fine river and site for water works. Have large experimental plant at site. Have made extensive studies. Would be a fine project but they have deferred it until later. Staff of girls ran the experimental plant. Had lunch on bank of river. Left about 4:30. Had 4 blowouts on way home. Arrived in Moscow about 9:30. Dinner at Savoy. Retired - felt rotten.

Tuesday, 10 Arose 7:30 & went with J.F.S. to Bessey's room in Savoy for breakfast to see if it was an improvement over the Europa. To water office city building at 9:30. Lunch there. Translated some of report on sewage. Left at 4. Wrote letter to Lil... received first letter from her - all well at home. Dinner at Savoy with Skinner. Spent evening until 9:30 in Mr. Seabrook's room - discussed situation. Returned to room & wrote a dozen postcards & retired.

Wednesday, 11 Arose at 7:30. Breakfast in Bessey's room at Savoy. Spent most of day until 4:30 in hotel room with Serge, our interpreter, translating sewage report. Bessey returned from Leningrad. Dinner at Savoy with him & Skinner. Walked about 2 miles in eve and stopped in a park (amusement). Saw a terrible moving picture. No ventilation - smell terrible. No decent movies in Russia apparently. No talking pictures. Retired about 11:30 - very tired.

Thursday, 12 Arose 7:30 a.m. Breakfast with Bessey at Savoy. Packed trunk to move out to Seabrook apartment. Trunk was supposed to be there at 10 a.m. Never arrived until 8 p.m. Spent most of day in room at Europa translating sewage report. Rode out in truck with trunk at 9 p.m. to apartment. Long ride - disappointed in arrangement. Still have to share room with Skinner. Found hot water in individual boiler in bath room and took a bath. Retired about 11.

Friday, 13 Arose 7:30 am. Slept well. Stomach better. Had good breakfast at apartment. Serge arrived about 10:30, and spent day until 4:30 translating water report. Translation very slow. Left apartment about 4:45 and took 1 hour to reach Savoy. Trolleys crowded. Dinner at Grand with Bessey & Skinner. Went to theater at 7:30 and saw ballet *Red Poppy*. Very interesting. Trolleys jammed, and finally got taxi to get back to apartment. Had circus, making taxi driver understand destination. Retired about 11 p.m.

Saturday, 14 Arose 8 a.m. Shy on breakfast at apartment. Coffee like dishwater. To Seabrook office on trolley, took 1/2 hour. Worked in a.m. at Seabrook office. Like bedlam, impossible to accomplish much. Lunch at Savoy with Bessey and Skinner. Bessey leaves for two week trip North to Arctic Circle this eve. Returned to apartment at about 3 p.m. Took an hour to get there. Worked on assembling information and start of brief report. Supper with married couple. Chatted till 10 p.m. - retired.

Sunday, 15 Worked all day translating water reports. Skinner at office getting letter typed.

Monday, 16 Worked all day at apartment till 6:30 translating project reports. Meals at apartment. No breakfast except kassa. Lunch fair. Supper pretty good. Went to Savoy at 8:30 to see Mr. Seabrook & discuss program. Skinner there. Read his letter to Mr. Gillespie. Has no idea of cooperation. Self interested. Relations very unsatisfactory. Went to work only by himself. From present indications will be able to get back home by middle of July - will not be sorry. Accommodations poor. Food miserable. Long ride on trolleys - always crowded to apartment.

Tuesday, 17 Arose 7 a.m. No eggs again for breakfast. Kassa - fine food. To Seabrook office then to Water Trust office at 10 a.m. More data on water works. In eve went to Russian Art Theater with Skinner. Cost 6.20 rubles. Saw play - *Three Fat Men*. Propaganda play with triumph of Prospero - workers. Long show - 7:30 to 11:30. Home to apartment about 12:15. Acting good - grotesque. Had no supper - only 2 cups of tea and 2 pieces poor cake. Cost 2 rubles. (inspected laying 36" pipe).

Wednesday 18 To office at 8:45. Kassa and 3 boiled eggs for breakfast - a little better. To water office for part of a.m. & p.m. getting data on water consumption & meters, and on Volga Project. Terrible lunch with Serge & Skinner at some greasy dump. To apartment at 5 o'clock. Jammed in like sardines. Wrote letter to Lil in eve.

Thursday, 19 To office at 8:45. To Water Trust office in a.m., and in p.m. to mayor's office with Mr. Seabrook. Mayor not in. Worked on collecting data for report. Same in eve at apartment.

Friday, 20 To Water Trust office at 9 a.m. Prepared for trip to Volga. Delay in starting, and had conference with Mr. Seabrook at mayor's office with mayor's representative re our program and commission of experts. Finally got off to Volga at 11 o'clock. Commissar of Water & Canalization Trust and Mr. Gooshine accompanied. Old touring car - about 12-13 years old. Distance about 75 miles, over Moscow-Leningrad highway. Highway about 100 meters right of way. Paved about 5 or 6 meters. Poor road. Wonderful possibilities for new concrete road. Straight as an arrow for most of way. Many miles lined with beautiful forests. Pine and white birch. Stopped at a large lake on way. Great fishing & duck shooting. Lake connected with a canal system built 100 years ago to connect Leningrad with Moscow, from Volga, but never completed. Saw canal. Weather rainy & cold at start, but cleared at noon. Last 20 k.m. over wide open fields. Houses on highway typical Russian log houses. Caravan of funny wagons, about 20, loaded with dishes, as we neared Volga. All horses afraid of automobile. Several ran away, one overturned with dray. Took pictures. Lunch in woods before we reached Volga. Nice lunch, red & white wine & vodka, bread, cheese, roast beef, veal, radishes, honey cake, etc. Fine picnic.

Volga River near Gorodisha – Peasant Caravan   *Peasant wagon upset along the Volga River near Gorodisha*

Commissar & Gooshine good fellows. Commissar followed a big pheasant which flew up 3 feet away. Many birds. Very pretty river. About 250 ft. wide +/- here. Had tea in peasant's house at village Gorodiska. Primitive living. No furniture except bed and benches. About 50 children around auto, and wanted a ride. Gave them kopeks. Left about 6. On way back, at city called Kleen, stopped for an hour at home of Tchaikovsky, great Russian composer. He lived here 2 years. Born in Ural mountains in 1840, died in 1893. House fixed up as museum. Very interesting. Reached apartment about 11 p.m. On way home a brown fox ran across the road in front of auto into forest.

Saturday, 21 Longest day of year. Moscow went on daylight saving time. Turned clock ahead 1 hour. Time now 7 hours ahead of Phila. daylight saving time. Wrote letter to Lillie (sister) in eve.

Sunday, 22 To Water Trust office at 9. Left about 9:30 with Commissar Kanyguine and chief engineer Gooshine. Skinner, Serge & chauffeur for trip to Upper Moscow and Ruza River. Long trip - weather cloudy & cold. had sweater, overcoat & raincoat on. Interesting trip. Long ride - about 175-200 miles. Inspected sites for proposed dams & impounding reservoirs. Ruza old town. Saw great earth wall, still standing, built to repel invasion of Tartars in 14th century. Went to Borodino battle field where Napolean defected Russian Army in 1812, on invasion to Moscow. Spent some time in museum. Many relics - caretaker gave me a small cannon ball found in field. Had lunch picnic in woods. Fine lunch. Vodka, red & white wines, konyak. Commisar & engineer seem to enjoy these parties. Picked wild flowers.

ISW front left

From left: Serge (interpreter), Chauffeur, Mr. Gooshine, Commissar Kanyguine

In eve had tea and more lunch in peasant's home, in a little village. Very primitive. Chickens & cows, etc. live in barn adjoining. Drank much hot tea with red wine. Excellent drink on cold day. Exciting time passing horses, all afraid of car. 4 or 5 ran away. One went over ditch and threw peasant woman out on her back. Our driver did not even stop. Saw 8 or 10 in front of homes. Some around big bonfires & seem to enjoy life. Arrived at apartment about 1 a.m. Gas line on carburetor broke, & chauffeur repaired it with a piece of rubber tile. Good machine.

Monday, 23 Worked all day in apartment on blocking out report. Serge arrived about 1 p.m. Translated until 5. Supper with men in eve. Wrote a bit more on report in eve. Retired about 11 p.m.

Tuesday, 24 Worked all day in apartment. Serge came at 10 a.m. Translated water report until 6 p.m. Had good dinner tonight. Good soup, goolash, potatoes and stewed strawberries & coffee. A new man in charge of apartment. Took a walk with Skinner through Siemenosky Fortress, across from apartment. Wonderful old time fortress. Monastery on hill overlooking river. Holes to shoot out of and pour out molten lead. Wrote letter to Lil in eve.

Wednesday, 25 Worked all day in apartment. Translated another water report - letters & tables only... also notes on all plans. Wrote some postcards, and letter to G. W. Fuller in eve.

Thursday, 26 To Seabrook office at 9 a.m. Finished letter to G. W. Fuller. To Water Trust office at 11. Saw Mr. Gooskin re additional data. Walked to office of official in charge of Kremlin & arranged to visit Kremlin at 12 o'clock Sunday - cost 3 rubles. Left office about 5:30 to go to apartment and found all cars, buses and taxis stopped on account of big parade celebrating the 16th conference of the Communist Soviet. Started to rain heavily, and had to walk a mile in the rain. Found it impossible to get h Mr. Hitchcock. Got home about 9:30.

Friday, 27 To office of Water Trust at 9 a.m. Took another trip to Rubleva plant with one of the engineers, configuration and .... dam, low region dam. Had dinner at Grand Hotel with Russia engineer & Mr. Hitchcock. Cost 42 rubles with tip for 5. Walked around town a bit in White City trying to find a department store I saw there one night, but couldn't locate it. Returned to apartment about 4:30, took a nap. Supper. Wrote to Mary & George & retired about 11 p.m.

Cake alum used in filtration
J.F. Skinner & Supt. at Rubleva Filter Plant

New Pre-filters at Rubleva

Saturday, 28 At apartment all day. Serge arrived 10 a.m. Translated on water report. Spent evening until 9:30 with men in Miskelly's room... mandolin. Wrote on data for an hour & retired.

Sunday, 29 Arose 8 a.m. Wrote report for brief period. Left at 11 with Skinner & Milligan for V.O.K.S. office. At 1 o'clock finally passed through gates of Kremlin, with guide - girl interpreter... wonderful experience. On avenue near entrance, 875 cannons captured from Napoleon in 1812. Museum in old armory building. Wonderful priceless collections. Remarkable that they were preserved during revolution. Priceless relics and collections of tsar's gold, silver, jewels and treasures from monasteries. Visit about 2 hours. Went with Skinner & Milligan. Lunch in Grand Hotel. Took walk with Milligan at river, and saw nude men & women bathers. Rather disgusting. Went through the Church of the Redeemer - biggest in Moscow. Took 45 years to complete. Most magnificent thing I ever saw. Home in eve.

Monday, 30 Arose 8 a.m. Wrote until 11:30. Met Serge at office at 1 p.m. and went to steamship office for record of sailings on different lines. Went to museum of Russian Handwork, and spent 40 rubles on some things to take back home. Returned to apartment for supper. Wrote to Lil & Charles McGough in eve.

JULY

Tuesday, 1 In rooms in a.m. Went to Seabrook office in p.m. to meet mayor with Mr. Perelatrius, but he was out. Went with Serge & Skinner to store and purchased $25.00 of old stuff to take home - old items... beaded bag, etc., czar's wine glass. Home in apartment in eve. Wrote to Jess Giesey.

Wednesday, 2 In rooms all day, writing up note on water situation.

Thursday, 3 To office after lunch. Bessey returned from trip up north. Went with him & Serge to store to get purchases made on July 1 & certificate. Then drove in droshki to Russian art museum and spent about 3 hours there. Wonderful exhibition of Russian paintings. Had supper at Grand with Bessey. Took a walk then home about 11 p.m. Met Mr. Hoski, the Polish American who we met on train to Moscow.

Friday, 4 All Seabrook organization took holiday. Spent day at rooms. Water data. Read cablegram about 10:30 last night from Gillespie to return home as soon as we secured the necessary data, but before August, or when Seabrook returns... that he might call us at Berlin to go to England to investigate some ....

Saturday, 5 To office in a.m. Went to office of Water & Sewage Trust, 11 to 1. Advised leaving on Monday. Said could not take maps, documents or reports out. Seabrook to send by mail. Made arrangement with George Perelatrius to leave Monday night. To rooms at 5:30. Packed trunk in eve.

Sunday, 6 Up 7:15. Went to church at 9 a.m. at Church of Christ. Found did not start until 10. Had some high priest there. All stand. All formal and ceremony. Motley gathering. Four priests - 3 and high priest. 3 or 4 assistants. Singing fair. Great display of golden relics. Following church visited Academy of Fine Arts. Wonderful building & exhibits of sculpture & paintings... old time relics. Back to office at 3. Left at 4 to do some shopping. Caught in heavy rain. Boarded trolley in rain about 4:45 for apartment. Trolley stopped. At end of 4 hours, circled around and landed back in center city, near Savoy. Young girl on car helped me to find way home. Spoke English. Took about 5 cars, and finally arrived at apartment about 10:30. No supper.

Monday, 7 Truck and car were due to come to apartment for luggage at 10 o'clock. All packed. Never showed up until nearly 12. Visited Mayor Boutozoff with Mr. Perlatrius to secure his certificate to leave Moscow and take necessary papers, plans & reports. Spent all day around office waiting for railroad tickets, visas, etc. So much red tape - much confusion getting trunk. Weighed 130 k.g., and got a husky Russian laborer to help, and he carried it down 5 flights, 97 steps, alone, on back. Charged 6 rubles. About 4 p.m. railroad tickets arrived & went to railroad station. Too late for Customs examination in Moscow, and will have to chance it at Niejerola. May hold up reports, etc., maps in box. To Savoy Hotel, and went to Grand for dinner with Bessey. Met George Perelatrius. Pretty good dinner with wine, vodka & caviar. Cost 45 rubles without tip. Charged 20 rubles for caviar for 4. Left for Berlin at 9:30 with Skinner & George Perelatrius - first class sleeper. Shared room with George Perelatrius. Slept O.K.

Tuesday, 8 Fair breakfast on train. Arrived Niejerola about 11 and went thru Customs. Some job. Passed all baggage O.K. but bad job about money. Had certificate stating we had lived on rubles from Seabrook during stay. Thought they were going to take away our money, but finally passed us. George Perelatrius was carrying about $1400 and they took all his money, American & English bills, except $107, and 2 travelers checks for $50 cash. Some government. Went thru Polish Customs at Stolpce, and had pretty good dinner at station. Arrived Warsaw about 9 p.m. and stopped for an hour. Took a stroll thru station with Perelatrius when two Poles accosted us wanting us to take a taxi ride for 3/4 hour thru the city. Forgot our visa was for transit only. Were considering it when a detective came up and hauled us into the police captain's office at station, & demanded to see passports. About 10 police in room. Advised us two taxi men were thieves and would probably have robbed us if we had gone with them. Some experience. Met very small English gentleman named Richards on train. Got good accommodations, first class sleeper from Niejerola in French car wagon lit. Bunked with Skinner. Good supper on Polish train.

Wednesday, 9 Pretty good breakfast. Arrived Berlin about 10 a.m. Lebarsky met Perelatrius at station Friedrichstrasse Bahnhof. Went to Adlon. Got nice room with Skinner. Went to English Consul & got visa to visit England. Cost $10.50. Back to Adlon for lunch. Wonderful meal and service after Moscow. First real meal for over 5 weeks. Wrote letter to Lil after lunch. Spent most of afternoon looking up steamers and tickets. Booked passage on S.S. New York, Hamburg American Line from Cherbourg-Southampton on July 19th, arriving 26th. Cost $320 each. Skinner bought German caviar. Supper Adlon. At 9 o'clock went to the Gloria Palast and saw *der Blaue Engel*. Received cablegram from Gillespie to go to London and interview Charles F. Lumb at Malaya House, Admiralty Arch re new patented material for building roads called ABC, & get back in New York for conference with Seabrook on July 28th.

Thursday, 10 Birthday. Breakfast about 9. Packed suitcase. Chatted with gentleman in lounge. Got reservation for trip to London. Taxi to Friedrichstrasse Bahnhof and left for London at 1:02 p.m. via Hook of Holland. German compartment car very fine. Interesting trip through Germany and Holland - intensive farming. Saw quite a few large Dutch windmills... a few people in wooden cabots. Excellent meals on train, both in Germany & Holland. Had fine old Muenchner beer & wine, small bottle white wine for 38 cents. Again met Mr. Richards on train, also English woman with small son traveling from China thru Russia to England, who was held up in Moscow due to accident... boy in hospital due drunken lorry driver. Passed thru quite a few cities... Utrecht, Rotterdam, outskirts of Amsterdam. Arrived Hook of Holland at 11:20 p.m. and boarded Channel steamer. Small single stateroom, very comfortable.

Friday, 11 Got up about 5:45 a.m. Steamer arrived at Harwich, England about 6 a.m. Channel crossing not bad. Passed thru British Customs. Inspection perfunctory, but very inquisitive re passports. About 40 or more miles from Harwich to London. Arrived London at Liverpool St. station about 8 o'clock, and took taxi to Grosvenor House. Very fine hotel. Got fixed up with room about 10 o'clock. Mr. Charles Lumb phoned about 10 a.m. and we called on him at his office - Malaya House, Admiralty Arch. He took us to office of company promoting ABC paving material. Met Captain W.S. Stephenson and partner Mr. Haywood, also Chief Engineer Mr. Gunvell. Made us familiar with the proposition. Apparently a remarkable paving material and useful for many other purposes. Had tea and drink in office. Mrs. Stephenson arrived about 7. Invited us to Hotel Grosvenor for dinner. Capt. & Mrs. Stephenson, Mr. Haywood, Skinner & self. Had fine dinner. About 10:00 Mr. Haywood took us to Murray Club. Home about 2:30.

Saturday, 12 Mr. Gunvell called for us about 10 a.m. Drive to Acton to see stretch of road paved with ABC, also test section of concrete road surfaced with it and other material. ABC only one left after 2 years. Drove to Hanworth airfield. Inspected floor of aerodrome laid with ABC. Lunch at club... fine old house recently utilized for air field. Gunvell arranged a flight for us and we had a wonderful trip in the air over London for 3/4 hour. Thriller for first flight. Traveled about 90-95 miles per hour. Wonderful experience. Driver told us many points of interest. Circled for 10 minutes over Henley course on Thames and saw boat races. Back to Capt. Henderson's office about 4. Discussed ABC, etc. over cocktails. To hotel... dressed. Capt. & Mrs. Stephenson called for us at 8:10 and took us to old Duke of York's Theatre and saw an English play, *The Way to Treat a Woman*. Four principal male characters were an English, a German, Italian & American detective. American fellow had decided English accent. Back to hotel - some cocktails & retired.

Sunday, 13 Slept late. Breakfast in room. Capt. & Mrs. Stephenson called for us at 2 o'clock in fine car with uniformed chauffeur, and drove us about 50 miles out in country through Surrey. Beautiful drive along Thames and countryside. Called on a cousin of Skinner's who runs a hotel in small town in Surrey. Much traffic. Thousands of people picnicking, boating, etc. Back to London about 8, and had wonderful dinner with champagne in Trocadero Restaurant, largest in world. Wonderful hosts. To hotel about 1:30.

W.B. Gunvell & J.F. Skinner after our flight over London

Capt. & Mrs. Stephenson in Surrey

Monday, 14 Up 8:30. Breakfast in room. To Capt. Stephenson's office at 10:45. To Birmingham on train 12 o'clock with Mr. Gunvell to inspect some flooring being laid with ABC in factory there. Rained. Clear to Stratford-on-Avon & had intended to go there but rain interfered. Lunch on train. Returned on 4:50 train & back to London at 7 p.m. To office, and after cocktails and old 1812 brandy, Capt. Stephenson took us to Kit Kat, famous cabaret. Mr. Gunvell & Haywood in party. Wonderful dinner with champagne, etc. Good entertainment. Left about 1:30 to hotel.

J.F. Skinner with Captain & Mrs. Stephenson

ISW with Mrs. Stephenson

Tuesday, 15 Up 8:30. Breakfast downstairs. Walked about town. Did some shopping. Arranged for French visas and airplane tickets. Called on Mr. Lumb. Called on Mr. Stephenson at 1. Had final talk on ABC. Capt. & Mrs. Stephenson entertained us at American Women's Club for lunch. Wonderful old home for clubhouse. Fine lunch with sparkling burgundy. Said goodbye to them at 3:30. Had quite a chat with Capt. Stephenson. To airways office at 4:05, and off for airfield by bus at 4:10. To Croyden airfield, boarded our plane, the "City of Manchester"... monster 3 engine plane. Left promptly at 5 p.m., reached Paris, 225 miles, at 7:17. Fine trip, cloudy at start, but cleared up.

Log of trip -- left London 5 p.m. Tonbridge 25 miles 5:12 - clear. Dungeness - English Channel 60 miles - 5:35. Altitude 2500 ft. LeTouquet 105 miles - 6:00 p.m. End of Channel. Abbeville - 135 miles - 6:24 p.m. Poix - 161 miles - Beauvais - 180 miles - 6:55 p.m. Beaumont 210 miles - 7:07 p.m. Paris - 225 miles - LeBourget flying field - 7:17 p.m.

Inspected at Customs - no examination. Bus to city office. Taxi to Hotel Lutetia. Secured nice room for $3.60 per day. Took walk with Skinner. Had supper at restaurant. Retired about 10 a.m.

Wednesday, 16 Breakfast at Lutetia. Bus to American Express office. Cashed travelers checks for $100. To Hamburg American Line - secured tickets for passage & railroad to Cherbourg. Paid embarkation fee. Left Skinner. Made some purchases in stores - neckties, bracelet, etc. Returned to hotel & changed clothes. Taxi to town in p.m. Dinner in restaurant. At 9:15 took American Express sightseeing trip around Paris. Raining. Only 6 in party. Met Mr. & Mrs. Broch, an elderly couple with granddaughter. Visited 5 cabarets. Danced at Moulin Rouge & others. Cost $6.40. Very interesting. Retired 2 a.m.

Thursday, 17 Breakfast at Lutetia. Friend of Skinner's, Madame LaGarde, called at Lutetia. Took us on sightseeing trip in taxi. Lunch in quaint French restaurant in Montmartre. Visited Cathedral of Sacred Heart. Rain all day. Visited Napoleon's Tomb, Louvre... saw daVinci & Mona Lisa, Statue of the Winged Victory, Venus de

Milo, etc. Met poet friend of Madame LeGarde, Mr. Bonelli, who gave us tickets for review featuring Raquel Miller. Fair. Had dinner at restaurant. To hotel about 12 a.m.

Friday, 18 Madame LaGarde called and went on train to Soissons. Skinner's friend, Miss Kate Gleason, maiden lady 65, met us at station in auto. Eccentric lady - very wealthy. Showed us battlefields, damaged houses, cathedral, caves, trenches, etc. at Bergy le Sec - scene of heavy fighting during World War. Took us to her home, an old chateau of 6th century. Had fine dinner. Coffee in attic... with old furniture.

Miss Gleason's Chateau
Setpmonts Aisne, France

ISW on roof of chateau
Old castle in rear

Returned to Paris in auto. Very interesting ride through battlefields. Quaint old French villages. Towns Soissons, Vierzy, Bergy le Sec, Boulevard Jeanne d'Arc, Avenue Chateau Thierry, Longpont Pontercher, Jaulzy, Breuel, Compiegne, Couldresy, Lamotte, Trochy, Armichia, Ralentia. Stopped to see old castle in Compiegne. Napoleon married there. Saw place where Jeanne d'Arc was captured & burned. Military graveyard where 17,000 French soldiers buried. Returned to hotel at 7:30 & changed clothes. Party at opera. Miss Gleason, Madame LaGarde & daughter, Mrs....., woman reporter, who was in issue for *McCall*'s magazine, Skinner & self. Skinner had to go up to balcony account of light suit. Saw *Rigoletto*, followed by ballet *Coppelia*. Pierre Nougaro - Rigoletto, Madam Eidi Norena sang Gilda. Very fine. Retired 12 a.m.

Saturday, 19 Up 6:30. Checked out of Lutetia, and taxi to station. Boarded train for Cherbourg. Arrived 3:30. Tender to boat S.S. New York. Met the Haights, also Mr. Felton on train. Have table on S.S. New York with them. Supper on boat at 8. Turned clock back 1 hour at start. Watched dancing & retired at 12.

S.S. New York nearing Cherborg Harbor

Sunday, 20 On board S.S. New York. Received letter from Lil, forwarded from Moscow, also birthday card from Hannah & Harry Getty. Weather cloudy & windy. Rather rough. Spent all a.m. trying to straighten out expense account. Moving picture at 9 p.m. *Love in the Ring* with Max Schmeling. Wonderful meals & service.

Monday, 21 On Board S.S. New York. Weather cloudy & cold. Quite rough. Writing in a.m. Deck chairs in p.m. Horse races at 4 p.m. Lost $1.50. Dancing in eve with Mr. & Mrs. Haight. Retired 12:30. Clock back 49 minutes.

Tuesday, 22 Breakfast at 8:30-9:30. Weather clear and warmer. Boat newspaper says terrific heat wave at home. 111 degrees in Washington. Swim in pool in a.m. - not in p.m. Moving picture at 9 p.m. Smoking room with Mr. & Mrs. Haight until 12.

Wednesday, 23 Hazy but sun out - warmer. Breakfast 8:30. Swim in pool at 11. Read on deck in p.m. Costume ball in eve... very colorful affair. Very sociable crowd. Festivity still on at 2:30 when retired.

Thursday, 24 Up 8 o'clock. Spent some time on notes from ABC report. Swim in pool at 11. Captain's dinner in eve. Dining room very pretty. Waiters in scarlet coats. Danced with Mrs. Haight. Opened little of old 1812 brandy.

Friday, 25 Bright & clear. Packed trunk in a.m. Removed from stateroom at 4 p.m. Swim in pool at 11:30. Wrote up some notes from ABC report. Finished book. No dress for dinner on last night. Sat on deck with Mr. & Mrs. Haight & Mr. Felton. Chatted for hour with Zimmer family. Reached Nantucket lights at 10 p.m.

Saturday, 26 Packed valise in a.m. Reached quarantine at 9:30. Docked at N.Y. about 11. Passed Customs examination in 1/2 hour. Expressed trunk home. Mrs. Skinner at wharf. Taxi to Hudson terminal. Caught 1:15 express for Atlantic City. Arrived 4:15. Bus to Ocean City, and to cottage - 849 St. James Place. Lil and children all well. Bob down from Wilkes-Barre - also Jule & Anna. Jule lost pocketbook with $40 in it. Walk on boardwalk in eve. Very hot day.

Sunday, 27 Cooler. Up about 9. Bathing from 12:30 to 4:30. Water cold and very dirty. Beach spoiled at upper part of island. Bathing with Pfizenmaiers, Tinsmans, Swensons, Wardles, etc. Mary & Grace Lockhart down.

Monday, 28 Up 5:30. Caught 6:20 train for Phila.-N.Y. Arrived Gillespie's office about 10:20. Conference. Lunch at Railroad Club. Discussion with Seabrook in p.m. Wanted report on sewage of Moscow. Skinner stopping at Commodore Hotel. Got room there and after supper worked until 1 a.m. on brief report for Seabrook & Gillespie on sewage.

Tuesday, 29 To Gillespie's office 9:30. Completed brief report and had it typed. Skinner working on high spots on water. Seabrook came over at 3 p.m. and had final discussion. Completed conference & business with Gillespie and left for Ocean City via Atlantic at 5 o'clock. Arrived at cottage about 9:30. Thunderstorm.

August 22, 1930

Mr. Thomas H. Gillespie, President
T. A. Gillespie Company
7 Dey Street
New York, New York

Dear Mr. Gillespie,

I beg to hand you herewith three copies of my final report on the Water Supply of Moscow, containing notes and memoranda on the present work, discussion of the proposed plans of development of the filters supply for Grater Moscow, and observations and recommendations therein.

Two of the copies contain a number of photographs which I took during my visit, of existing works on proposed sites.

I would suggest that you forward one complete copy to Mr. Seabrook with the thought that it might be useful in his future negotiating with the Moscow officials.

I am also handing you a set of the reports on the Moscow Water System, with heading and table translations as we were able to obtain, during our visit.

Yours very truly,

Isaac S.Walker

Mr. Thomas H. Gillespie, President
T. A. Gillespie Company
7 Dey Street
New York, New York

Gentlemen:

During the month of May 1930, Mr. John F. Skinner, Consulting Engineer of Rochester, N.Y., and the writer, were commissioned by your Company to visit Moscow, U.S.S.R., to study the water and sewer facilities of the City. On May 21st, we left for Russia, arrived in Moscow on May 31st, and spent six weeks there in surveys and studies of the problems.

Following our arrival in Moscow, our first ten days were spent in a visitation to existing works, and proposed water supply sites, in accordance with a program arranged by the Engineers in Charge. Later, we also visited several more of the proposed sites for future water supply.

We held numerous conferences with the Water and Canalization (Sewerage) Engineers, in the endeavor, in the limited time available, to familiarize ourselves with the proposed plans of development. In both Departments we have been impressed with the technical skill of the designers, and supervising engineers and chemists, and with the exhaustive study given to the comprehensive plan of extensions, as well as maps, plans, descriptions, and other necessary engineering and analytical data on existing works. In general, the data has been promptly furnished.

With this complete information at hand, our task would have been greatly lightened, if either of us were conversant with the Russian language. The translation of technical reports is time consuming, and in such translations, as well as in conferences with the engineers through an interpreter, there is always the possibility of errors and misunderstandings.

Following is a brief citation of certain notes and memoranda collected by the writer, in connection with the present and future water supply of Moscow, together with some discussion of the proposed plan of development by the city authorities, and observations and recommendations therein.

CITY IN GENERAL

Moscow is the capital and the largest city of the Soviet Union (U.S.S.R.). It lies near the center of the East European plain, 55 degrees 45' N, latitude, and 37 degrees 31' E. Longitude, on the Moscow River. It is the greatest center of industry and trade, with textile, leather, metal and foodstuff industries predominating.

The average yearly temperature is about 50o F. The winters are severe lasting about 5 months and are followed after a brief spring, by a hot summer. The average annual rainfall is about 540 millimeters, or 21 inches, as shown by records of the past 35 years. In dry years the total annual fall may not exceed one half of the average. Most of the total fall occurs in one month.

The population in 1929 according to the Water Department figures, was about 2, 500.000. The city is exceeding its boundaries rapidly, and a population of over 4,000,000 is anticipated by 1950, within the present limits of the ring railroad.

The city, which dates from about the year 1147, has grown in a series of concentric zones around the inner walled city, with encircling boulevards and streets. In 1917 the limits of the city were extended include the suburbs lying beyond the former boundary of the KammerKollezhahy Wall, and now in general terminate at the ring railroad. These limits have a diameter of approximately 10 miles covering an area of about 81 sq. miles. It is anticipated that by 1950, the limits will extend to a diameter of about 30 square miles, with a population of about 6 million.

The surface of the city is moderately hilly with elevations above mean sea level ranging from 123 to 165 meters. Many of the streets are broad avenues. Much of the paving in the city consists of cobblestones, which is rapidly being replaced in many sections with asphalt. There are about 750 miles of streets, of which about 400 miles are paved.

ORGANIZATION

Control of the water and sewage of the City is vested in the Water and "Canalization Trust," under the Communist Government of Moscow, with the following personnel:

Commissar V. E. Kanyguine, Chairman of the Trust
Mr. N. J. Gooschine, Chief Engineer of Water Works
Mr. J. J. Zwjaguinsky, Chief Engineer of Canalization (Sewerage) Professor S. N. Stoganov, Chemist
Mr. L. A. Alifata, Asst. Engineer on Canalization
Mr. Bodkovsky, Asst. Engineer on Water Works
Mr. Krondrashov, Project Engineer, Water Works
Mr. S. Ozerov, Sanitary Chemist
Mr. A. Prudnchov, Asst. Chief Engineer, on Water Works
Mr. Serge Souvorov, Interpreter

GENERAL ORGANIZATION OF SYSTEM

About 90% of the present water supply is obtained from the Moscow River, at a point about 31 miles above the center of the city, measured along the winding course of the stream. The intake main pumping station and filter plants are located near the village of Rubleva, about 11 miles from the City Center by air line. The water is effectively filtered by a system of double filtration, and pumped to a distribution reservoir situated on Vorobiesky hill near the Moscow River where it is distributed to the city. The reservoir is about 5 miles southwest from the city center. About 18 million pails per day are furnished for present demand from Ruvbleva. Total available for withdrawal for water supply from unregulated run about 20 to 21 million pails per day.

The other 10% of the supply is obtained from a series of driven wells at Mitishensky. From these wells the water is lifted to a reservoir at the Oldenborg High Duty Pumping Station, from where it is pumped to two elevated tanks known as Krestovsky Towers, in the city, and distributed. The wells are about 12 miles from the city center. They furnish about 2 million pails or 6.5 mgd.. Total present supply to city from both sources, about 20 million pails per day (=65 mgd.)

WELL SYSTEM

Brief History: The first public supply was built about 150 years ago, during the reign of Catherine 2nd (The Great). Supply from large springs at Mitishensky. A large brick collector conveyed the water by gravity to a gravity lake or ford, from which it flowed to a distributing point in the city, across the Ruza River through the Rostokinsly Aqueduct. Remains of the brick collector still exist. (See Ill. 33. Page 62, 1929 Water Report.). The old aqueduct is still used to carry the cast iron pipes for the new supply. (See Ill. 34, Page 63.).

In 1826, the brick aqueduct broke, and the Alexii (now Oldenborg) Pumping Station was built at Soholinsky, from which the water was pumped through a cast iron pipe to a new tower in the city, known as the Suharev Tower. This tower, while not used, is still standing, and is used as a commercial museum. The tank on the tower was of cast iron, about 12,000 gallons capacity, and the water was distributed through a number of pipe fountains. The total supply was about 1 mgd.

In 1858, the springs became inadequate, and additional supply up to 1 2/3 mgd was obtained from wells. A steam pumping plant was built at Mitishensky to lift the water from the wells, from where it flowed by gravity in cast iron pipes to the Alexii Pumping Station, where additional pumps were installed.. At this time some 44 Verats (=29 miles) of cast iron pipe were laid in a city distribution system, and 26 street hydrants were installed. No water in the houses.

In 1870 the Water Works came under Municipal Control. The Mitishensky supply was inadequate and artesian wells were sunk in 3 other locations. (These are now abandoned).

Between 1880-1890, a plan was made to increase the total supply from Mitishensky wells to 10 million pails, or 32 mfd., but it was found the quality could not be attained, and the project was limited to 3 1/2 million pails or 10.5 mgd. By 1892, the supply was increased to about 5 mgd. The number of wells were increase to 50, and two imposing distribution towers (Krestovsky Towers) were built in the city. There were about 38 miles of pipes in the distribution system at this time.

Sewers were laid in the city in 1898, which increased the demand for water, and in 1902 the supply was increased to the powered maximum of 10.5 mgd, by the addition of 20 drilled wells, and additional steam pumps. The pumping of this quantity lowered the ground water table, increased the cost of operation, and the hardness quality increased.

It became evident that the supply was limited, and that 10.5 mgd could not be continuously be withdrawn. In 1895 the question of a new source of supply arose, and in1898 researches began for a source from the Moscow River.

With a supply available from the Moscow River, no further extensive development of the ground water system has been made, other than the electrification of the Mitishensky station in 1929, and of the Oldenborg Station in 1926. The present supply of well water from Mitishensky is limited to about 2 million pails 6 1/2 mgd. It supplies the highest elevation of the city, and the sections most distant from the distributing reservoir of the Moscow River system.

Present System Wells

Water collection area about 75 square km, = 29 sq miles, on the watershed of Ruza River. Water carrying sands about 7 meters deep. Twenty (20) driven wells, 16' dram; 90 to 100 feet deep, on right bank of Ruza River. All 20 on a line about 600 meters (about 2000 feet) long. Wells connected by 8 inch c.i. branches to the 24' c.i. Main collecting pipe, and pumped from main pumps in station. Wells equipped with individual deep well pumps, capacity 250,000 pails per day. Pharso make (German) Not used at present. (See insert No. 2, 1929 Report for cross section).

Mitishensky Station

See insert #, 1929 Report for layout plan, also illustration 21 to 27 inclusive. Pumping equipment 2 Electric Motor operated centrifuge pumps, direct connected. Installed in 1924. Capacity 2,100,000 pails per day each. 200 H.P., 220 volts. Electric current supplied from central Moscow District State Electric Station, at 6500 volts. Pumps set at low level in station building, about 6.5 meters below ground floor. Motor operated vacuum pumps. Gage registered 55 cm (22") vacuum, at time of visit.

Former steam pumps, with a 5 million pails pumping capacity are maintained as reserve. Electric pumps have effected savings in pumping costs. Station costs about 170 Rubles per million pails, excluding interest, with electric current at 4 kopeks per K.W.H. Similar conditions, with old steam pumps cost 320 Rubles.

Numerous buildings are located at the station, including store rooms and residences for operators.
From the Mitishensky wells, the water is furnished to the reservoir at the Oldenborg high lift station, through two 24' c.i. pipelines, about 14 km long.

Oldenborg Pumping Station

See Illustration No. 26, in 1929 Report.

High lift station. Water from Mitishensky low lift pumps enters covered reservoir at Oldenborger Station in aerating fountain. Capacity of reservoir 1.05 million pails. High left pumps take suction from this basin.

Equipment:
1 electric motor operated centrifugal pump. 300 H.P. capacity 2 million pails per day
1 electric motor operated centrifugal pump. 155 H.P. Capacity 1 million pails per day
Current 220 volts supplied from Central State Electric Station at 6500 volts.
Electric pumps installed in 1926. Old steam pumps held in reserve.
Three pumps triple extension. Two 2 million pails a per day capacity. One 1 1/2 million pails.
Electric high lift pumps deliver to two elevated tanks located in the city, known as Krestovsky Towers, 37 meters high, brick ornamental structure, tanks about 26 feet deep. Capacity of 2 tanks about 300,000 pails. Water level about elevation 75 meters above Moscow River Station. Two cast iron force mains from pumps to towers, about 2 verst (7000 feet) long. One 24' one 30".
An elaborate system of electric recording gages at the pump station indicates the water levels in the section reservoir and elevated tanks.

Main Repair Shops located at Pumping Station. Large machine shop, with about 60 different machines of best foreign made. Well operated and all work standardized. Meter shop for repairing all meters. See Ill #28, 1929 Report.

Well Supply in General

Supply from Miticshensky wells now limited to about 2 million pails per day, and supplies the highest district of the city, about 8 square kilometers in area, in the northern section as now supplied with water.

Normally the water is hard, about 250 P.M., and contains somewhat excessive amounts of iron & manganese, (see analyses appendix sheet). If an amount greater than 2 million pails per day is pumped, the hardness, iron & manganese increase. The water is crystal clear, and of uniform low temperature throughout the year, about 7 degrees C (45 degrees F). It is of high quality, free from bacteria, and is served to the city without treatment or chlorination.

A strict sanitary zone is maintained in the vicinity of the Mitischensky Wells. Guards are on duty at all stations, and the public is excluded.

Some troubles from iron deposits in the distribution system are experienced from the supply. Consideration has been given to iron removal, but as the supply is so small in comparison with the entire city supply, it is felt that the expense is not warranted. Furthermore, with the increase in the Moscow River supply, the areas now served from Mitischensky will be more generally served from the river source, and the well supply utilized for the growing suburban districts in the vicinity of the wells and pumping station.

The 24' and 30' force mains from Oldenborg to Krestovsky Towers have capacity in excess of 2 million pails per day and to utilize this capacity to better advantage, a driven well, 240 meters deep, has recently been completed at Oldenborg, equipped with a ventricle centrifuge pump, electric motor, 600 H.P. 3 phase, delivery approximately

1/2 million pails per day. The water from the well flows to the reservoir at the station, where it is mixed with the Mitischensky well water and pumped to the city.

Another similar well is proposed, which will bring the total of ground water supplied to the city, from Oldenborg Pumping Station, through Krestovsky Towers, to about 3 million pails per day (9.75 mgd).

Moscow River

Source of Moscow River in the Province of Smolensk, about 100 miles west of Moscow. Runs through Province of Moscow for length of about 280 miles. Flows into the Oka River at Kolomno, about 70 miles SE of Moscow. Principal tributaries before Moscow, Ruza and Estra Rivers. Total watershed area above water works intake at Rubleva, about 7350 square km (2840 square miles) See sketch No. 1, Page 44, Vol. 2, 1929 Report. Researchers. Minimum flow usually in February. Maximum in April, from melting snow and ice, when great floods usually occur. River at low water about 60 meters wide. Banks clay. River carries high turbidity during freshet. Bottom generally sand & gravel deposits. Considerable population on watershed. Requires careful filtration.

Brief History of Water Supply Works

Researches for supply from river, begun in 1898. Project started in 1900. Works located near village of Rubleva, 50 km along river above Moscow. River very winding. 15 km by road. Site well isolated. Special Water Works Commission organized for planning of works and control of sources. Still exists. Sanitary zone established. First installment 3.5 million pails per day. Successive gradual increases to 21 million pails per day. First installation sedimentation basins and slow sand filters. River water enters intake well, is pumped by low lift pump to sedimentation basins, flows by gravity through filters to clear well & lifted by high lift pump to distribution reservoir on Variobesky Hill.

Slow sand filters clogged during high turgid periods, and by 1912 pie filters were added, coagulation introduced, Variobesky reservoir increased by 2 million pails and new pumps and boilers added to provide plant output of about 7 million pails per day. In 1917, new pie and slow sand filters were installed, 2 diesel pumps added, and capacity increased to 10.5 million pails per day. In 1925 the pumping station was partly electrified, and full equipment can handle 21 million pails per day, which is considered to be the maximum daily amount which can be withdrawn from Moscow River without regulation or impounding reservoirs. With recent plant additions, present filtering capacity is about 18 million pails per day, at normal rates. Additional filters are now being constructed. Consumption records for year ended Oct 1, 1929, showed an average of 19.9 million pails per day supplied to city. Of this about 2 million pails were from Mitischensky Wells, and 17.9 million pails from Rubleva. Regular chlorination of the Moscow River supply was begun in 1929.

Present Plant

Intake: Substantial intake structured. On Cairson, area about 230 sq. meters. Projects into stream about 3 meters. Water admitted through 2 rows of lime screen to protect pump suctions. 42' and 48'pipes to pumps. On opposite shore of river, 19 earth projections extend toward intake, in order to maintain deep channel at inlets.

Pumping Station

Two large brick buildings. One for steam pumps. Second building houses Diesel and Electric Pumps.
Steam Plant 13 Lancashire Boilers. 12 atmospheres Pressure Oil Fwd. 2 Babcock & Urleux
4 Hor. Triple Ex. Steam Pumps (Zoolzer) low lift.240 H.P. Capacity 4 million pails per day.
4 Ho. Triple Exp. Steam Pumps (Zoozler) high lift 567 H.P. Capacity 3 1/2 million pails per day.

2nd Bldg. 2 Diesel Motor. 3 cyl. 375 H.P. Built in Russia at Kalumna. Belt connected to 2 low lift centrifugal Pumps (Zoozler). Capacity 4.5 to 5.0 million pails per day. 435 R.P.M. 1 3/4 atmospheres.
2 Diesel Motor. 6 cyl. 750 H.P. 150160 R.P.M. Belt connected to 2 high lift centrifugal pumps (Zoozler). Capacity 3.5 million pails per day.
545 R.P.M. 7 1/2 atmospheres.
2 Electric Motor Operated Centrifugal Pumps. Single stage. Low lift. 400 H.P. 485 R.P.M. Pressure 1 4/4 to 2 atmosphere.
Capacity 5 million pails per day. Direct connected.
2 Electric Motor Operated Centrifugal Pumps. High lift. 2 stage 1100 H.P. 585 R.P.M. Pressure 7 1/2 to 8 atmospheres. Capacity 4 million pails per day each.
Total pumping capacity. Low lift. 36 million pails per day. High lift. 29 million pails per day.

Sedimentation Basins

Lowlift pumps lift water to six reinforced concrete covered basins. Each compartment 75 meters wide X 50 meters long X 4 meters deep. Volume 1,100,000 pails each. Total volume 6.6 million pails. Total area + 25,000 square meters. Normal capacity of basins 18 million pails per day, basin 10 hours retention period, with volume of flow 2 mm per second.

Coagulation used at times of high turbidity, always during fall rains and spring freshets. Sulphate of alumina used in amount up to 1 to 1 1/2 grains. Per pail (Equivalent to 4 3/4 to 7 grains per gallon). Normal transferences of river water about 230 c.m. Falls to 6 or 8 c.m. at high flows. Coagulation used when transferency is less than 100 c.c. chemical received at plant in large cakes. Ground in special grinder. Applied in solution. Dissolving in tanks assisted by air.

Prefilters

80 units. 5 meters wide x 17 meters long. 1,92 meters deep. Reinforced concrete. Total area 7,050 square meters. (Total area probably same area as dimensions given + 6800 square meters + 1.68 acres). 64 filters entirely under roof. Original 16 hard earth cover. One central wash water trough, lengthwise of filters, reinforced concrete. No transverse gutters. Strainer system, false bottom, reinforced concrete plates with small hoes. Air and water wash. Air pressure 1.9 meters water column. Filters usually air washed for 30 minutes. 5% wash water used. About 27 c.m. depth of gravel and 54 c.m. depth of sand, as below:

Gravel 8 to 16 mm. Gravel 4 to 8 mm. Gravel 2 to 4 mm Sand 1/2 to 1 mm
10 c.m. deep 10 c.m. deep 7 c.m. deep 54 c.m. deep
The surface of sand about 18 inches below trough level. Usual rate of filtration about 1 1/2 meters per hour - vertical. Capacity under normal conditions reported as 18.2 million pails per day = 65 Mgd. = Rate of approximately 40 million gallons per acre per day.
See illustrations 15 and 16, pages 20 and 21, 1929 Report.

Slow Sand Filters

22 units. Sand area each unit = 3,000 sq. meters = 3/4 acre. Total sand area = 66,000 sq. meters = 16 /3 acres. Depth of water 1 meter.

Strainer system false bottom over entire area. Reinforced concrete plates, with small holes, similar to the filters, but larger plates. 27 cm. Of gravel and 111 cm. of sand as follows in layers.
Gravel 8 to 16 mm 10 c.m. deep Gravel 4 to 8 mm 10 c.m. deep Gravel 2 to 4 mm 7 c.m. deep Sand 1 to 2 mm 4 c.m. deep Sand 0.3 to 1mm 107c.m. deep

Average rate of filtration about 150 mm per hour (vertical) = 1/10 of the pre filter rates = 4 M.G. per acre per day.

Total capacity at normal rates given as 17.7 million pails per day.
Effluent controllers located in collecting chamber. Special apparatus consisting of large flats, telescopic tube, with ports and shutters to regulate size of openings. Float maintains constant head on outlet orifices.
Loss of head run up to 900 to 1000 m.m. before cleaning. Hand scraping about 10 m.m. from surface. Removed in cars to storage in court adjacent to hopper series hand washer. All sand and gravel from Moscow River. Washed and graded at station.

Clear Well

Very small capacity. 1 million pails (3 1/4 mg.). Has been trebled in size since 1927. Formerly only 336,000 pails. About 4 meters deep. At entrance is fine inspection well. White tiled floor. Clear and green glass windows. Very effective.

Chlorinators

Chlorination begun in summer of 1929. 4 Ornstein (German) machines. Average dose about 0.3 mg per filter. (=2 1/2 lbs. Per million gallons). Applied at inlet to clear well. Liquid chlorine of Russian manufacturer used.

Tests for residual chlorine made every 2 hours. Residual. Of 0.05 P.M. maintained at eff. From clear well after 1 1/2 to 2 hours contact. If below, dose is increased.

From the clear well at Rubleva, high lift pumps deliver the filtered, chlorinated water through 4 36" c.i. pipelines to Voriobesky Reservoir. In addition there is a 5th 3.6" line extending to the NW section of the city, direct to the distribution systems.

Reservoir about 5 miles southwest of city. Situated on highest point of Varoba Hills. Covered reservoir. Brick and reinforced concrete Original section built in 1902, and gradually increased in 4 more installments. Present capacity 4,600,000 pails. Maximum depth 2 Sagenes = 14 feet. Divided into 2 separate basins. Elaborate inlet house, with water from pump station entering over 8 flared risers, followed by drop of about 3 to 4 feet over main well with full reservoir. Elevation of bottom about 75 meters above Moscow River datum.

This is the only distribution reservoir in city system, except Krestovsky Tanks. Very limited capacity. Site will allow extension up to 12 million pais. Will probably increase to 8 million pails, with additional storage elsewhere.

Distribution System

Ring plan. 30" & 36" main feeds in Sadova St. Encircling center city. About 2 2/3 miles drain f ring. Two 36" supply lines from Variobesky Reservoir, connect to ring in southern part of city. Another 36" connects to ring at the western part. A 36" branch from the main reservoir line extends around through the south and east section, and returns to the Sedova Ring on the north. The fifth line, previously referred to, runs direct from Rubleva Station, ties into the Sadova ring on the NW, and continues across the center and ties into the ring on the south. A sixth 36" main supply is now being laid from Rubleva Station, branching on the north, to complete the circuit of the city with an outer ring. On the north 2 28" lines carry Mitishensky well water from Krestovsky tanks to the Sadova Ring. This water is supplied in a closed system to the adjacent higher district in the north.
For the extension of the distribution system to the new limits of the ring railway, many miles of large supply lines will be required. Present total length of supply & distribution mains (928) = 725 Km. (Small table page 34, 1929 report) 50% 6" and 7" pipe. Present piped area about 100 square verats. Total area of city , inside the Ring RR = 186 square verats about 81 square miles. (See services)

All pipelines cast iron, except some steel river lines. Pipes laid 3 meters deep, on account of front penetration. Bridge crossing insulated. Lead used for joints. Generally no house connections made to large mains.

Pressures

Ground elevation varies from 8 to 50 meters along City Datum = Moscow River level. With the Varobewski Reservoir full, at elevation of 78 meters, the static pressure on the pipelines varies in different sections from 20to 70 meters, equivalent to 29 to 100 lbs per square inch. Elevation of full Krestovsky Tank 75 meters.

Fire Hydrants

Spacing good. Total number (1929 report) = 5300 located at street intersections, and 100 meters apart on long streets. Flush types, located generally in manholes. Portable by rent with hose outlets carried by fire or street departments, and screwed or bolted to riser in manhole, for use.

Gates

Street gates generally Ludlow type, installed in manholes Number of manholes, at end of 1928 9,400. Generally brick vaults, about 500 wood boxes, which are being replaced.

Services

See Table of statistics page 59, 1929 Report. 11770 services, at end of 1928 connected to water supply. 27,000 total number of premises in city. C.I. pipe required for all services generally 2". Total length of 11,770 service branch = 384 km. Makes average service 107 feet each. Great average length due to practice of one service, in many cases, being carried into courts., alleys, etc., and supplying numerous buildings, as one holding. Practice of Department also to lay the service lines in to the house meter. Depth of not less than 1 sagene, 7 feet required for service pipes, acct. deep front.

Meters

All water to consumers metered. Generally installed in buildings. A few in boxes. Total number reported in service as of March 1930 = 12,400. Total number owned, including new meters on hand, reserved for repair and about 2900 sub meters for tenants etc., about 17,765. Close follow up on meters in service. Tested every 2 3 years. In 1928, 5688 tested and charged.

All meters formally of French (Frage) Piston type. About 7500+ of this make. All meters now of German velocity type. Siemens & Meineche Compound.

General Plant Operational Control

Apparently skilled supervision and control of all departments. Total personnel about 900. All plants under strict guard. No outsiders admitted except by pass.

Sanitary zone established since 1915, to control pollution of Moscow River above Rubleva intake, for length of 80 km, and area of 2000 square meters.

All work of filtration under control of the laboratory, and sanitary physician of the station and the protective zone. Daily lateral logical analyses of raw, settled, prefiltered and final filtered effluents. Complete chemical analyses over a month. Partial chemical analyses every 5 days.

See analyses. P. 4850, 1929 Report, covering raw water and filtered effluent determination at Rubleva.

See Table, Page 286, Tom 2, Water Researches, for chemical analyses of Moscow River Water at Rubleva. Average 1914 to 1925.

See Tables, Pages 308 to end of book, Tom 2, Researches, for details of analyses, Moscow River, at Rubleva.

Problem of Additional Supply

Population and Water Consumption

Population figures vary somewhat, in different records. In 1916, population about 1,940,000, with daily consumption (in 1917) of 13.25 million pails per day. Following the economic disturbance, population greatly decreased, and in 1920 was only 1,120,000. A corresponding decrease in water consumption did not occur, however, due to leaks and inefficiency during general upheaval and revolutionary times. Since 1921, population has been rapidly increasing. According to figures furnished by the engineer in charge of statistics, the total water consumption, as checked for the year ended October 1, 1929, average 19.9 million pais per day. The total population of the city within the limits of the Ring railroad, was 2,423,500. Of this total, 2,185,000 received water service from the city system, including some 390,000 served by street hydrants for common use.

Classification Remarks
Industrial Plants Railroads

Distribution of Water Record as of October 1, 1929

Average Daily Consumption

Cubic Meters:
46,030 10,914

Pails Million U.S. Gallons Mill
3.75 12.15 0.89 2.88

Public Baths
Laundries
Population Served 156,622 12.79 water in street
NonMaterial (Fire Hydrants)
leakage, & unaccounted for 20,000 1.63 for
(Very low)
Total   243,955 19.9
            2.36 0.36
            64.5
            9,032
            1,357 0.11
            0.73

Above demand is equivalent to 8.21 pails per capita per day (=101 liters = 26.5 gallons) on basis of total population of 2,423,500.

The department figures an average of 1 pail per day per capita use, by the 390,000 served by street hydrants. On the basis of population using water through the pipe systems direct to properties, demand appears to be about 10.87 pails (=133 liters 35.2 gallons) per capita per day.

41.47 (2,185,000 using 5.28 = 8.2% unnecessary

See Table p.59 of 1929 Report, for statistics on development of water supply, and total per capita consumption for each year from 1890 to 1928. See also diagrams, pp 56, 57 & 58.

See Table Page 66, for forecast of population and water consumption from 1928 to1960. The department estimated by 1950 they must provide for a population of 4,380,000, 53.1/2 million pails per day average, equivalent to 12.2 pails (=150 liters = 39.5 gallons) per capita.

Total demand, 53.5 million pails = 173.5 mgd., in 1950. (See also Table No. 1, Page 41, of Tom 2, 1929 Researches. This provides for an increase in the average per capita rate of consumption of 49%, based on present use and total population, but only 12% considering the present population using water in homes and buildings.

This allowance of 39.5 gallons per capita, for 1950, is only about 1/3 to 1/2 the usual consumption in all metered American cities. Recent reconsideration has been given to the above published estimates and forecasts, and subsequent studies on water and sewage requirements for 1950, are based on substantial increase of above figures, considering future city outside of limits of ring railroad. It is anticipated that the future city of greater Moscow, will have a diameter of 50 KM , with a population, in 1950, of approximately 4 million, within the present ring railroad limits, and 2 million in the new outside zone. Future requirements based on a per capita allowance of about 250 liters (66 gallons) for the population within the ring railroad, and 100 liters (26 gallons) outside.

The following are latest (1930) estimates for basis of future water extensions.

Years Increase:
1930 31
1931 32
1 year
1932 33
1 year
1938 670,000 per year for 5 years 1943 900,000 per year for 5 years 950 1,150,000 per year for 7 years
Cubic Meters
Million Pails
25.2 30.2
34.6 54.6 73.4 93.6

Million Gallons %
310,000 370,000
82 98
112
177 12% 238 7% 304 4%
426,000
15% in

With a population of 6 million in greater Moscow, in 1950, the total of 93.6 million pails (304 mgd) will provide per capita consumption of 15.6 pails = 191 liters = 50 gallons per day.

New Sources Considered

The department considers the safe yield of the Moscow River, at Rubleva, to be 60 million pails per day. Of this minimum flow, 40 million pails per day are required to maintain navigation below Moscow, leaving 20 million pails per day available for water supply purposes.

Of the present reported daily consumption of 19.9 pails, about 17.5 million pails are taken from the river, the balance from Mitishensky wells together 20% in with a new driven well at Oldenburg. The consumption is therefore rapidly approaching the limit of the available river supply, and the need of a new source is practically imperative.

Many schemes have been considered, resulting in detailed studies of three principle projects as possible supplies for future Moscow, as follows:
1. The Volga River, on the North
2. The Oka River, on the South
3. The Moscow River

by increasing the safe yield for available water supply by the construction of 3 large impounding reservoirs on the upper river and two tributaries, with a possible fourth reserve reservoir on another tributary, releasing the necessary flow as required, down the stream channels to the station at Rubleva, controlling the flow by means of a roller lift dam across the river, about 2 km above the present intake.

NUMBER 1: THE VOLGA PROJECT

The Volga River is about 15 km distant from the center of the city, at it's nearest point north of Moscow. The low water level at proposed site is a trifle higher than the Moscow datum. The river is about 180 to 250 meters wide , and about 3 meters deep. Shores studied for a length of 75 km. 3 sites considered for location of pump station and filter plant. The western site preferred, near the village of Gorodiska. Other sites at Federofha and Nutroma. The Shosha River, a large tributary, enter the Volga just above Gorodiska. Minimum dry weather flow reported about 300 million pails per day. (One engineer stated 250 million pails).

Many marshes. None in vicinity of Gorodiska. Considerable navigation, extending 200 km above Gorodiska. Navigation maintained during summer low weather flows by means of reservoirs. Very old, built over 100 years ago. Even with these, navigation is stopped sometime for 1 1/2 to 2 months during very low years. If large amount is taken for water supply purposes, regulation will be required. Excellent route for pipelines, from Gorodiska to Moscow, along MoscowLeningrad railroad, and parallel with Leningrad paved road. Straight road. Width 120 meters. 5 or 6 meters width of paving. Railroad spur 9 km long. required to reach site of pumping station. Pumping station 3 km from the highway.

Some years ago, Department established an experimental plant to study the filtration of Volga River water. See analyses , Vol. 4, page 155.

Most objectionable feature is high color during low weather flows, particularly when water is released from navigation reservoirs, due to swamp drainage. A large quantity of coagulant would be necessary to remove color. Estimated 10 times more coagulant required than with Oka units.

Sand available for site for pumping station and filter plant. Cost about same as for Oka site. Pumping pressure 14 to 16 atmosphere, with one lift.

Pipelines figured on basis 30 million pails per day, same as Oka scheme. Diameter 1 1/2 meters, length 108.6 meters. Two lines, 15 million pails each.

A site for a reservoir is available on the divide, at elevation 115.2 meters, 31.6 km from the city, from which the flow can be gravity to the pumps at the city station.
Force main section 77 KM long = 253,000 feet. See Probable Insert 8. Vol. 2, Researches (gray book). Two lines, 1 1/2 meters diameter = 59".15 million pails each = 48.5 mgd.

60" pipe ©+ 120)has capacity of 48 mgd. With loss of 0.8' per 1000'. V + 3.94' per second. 0.8' x 253 + 202.4 feet total loss of head. Loss as shown on profile. Elevation 176.8 115.2 (Elevation w.l in reservoir)

NUMBER 2: THE OKA PROJECT

The Oka River is due South of Moscow, about 105 km distant from it's nearest point to the center of the city. Large watershed, about equal to Volga at proposed sites, minimum dry weather. Flow about 300 million pails per day. (One engineer stated 250 million).

Shore line studied for 150 km, and only possible sites available, one near the city of Kolomna at the mouth of the Moscow River, the other about 100 km upstream near the village of Volshovski.

Upper site (Volshovkos) chosen as most desirable, with less pollution. Lower site was first considered finally owing to good communication on level roads and railroad, and close proximity to two large electric power stations, interconnected to Moscow.

Upper site excellent for water supply. Fine river, about 200 300 meters wide. Alternately deep and shallow. 10 meters deep opposite site. Gravel formation on one side. Black earth on the other side. Some navigation on river. No population in vicinity of site. Village about 15 km upstream. Larger town about 60 km upstream. No swamps or marshes. Department erected large experimental plant at site, which has been operated continuously for over a year, but to be discontinued shortly.

Water of excellent quality. Limestone formation and water rather hard. B coli about 1/10 that of Moscow River at Rubleva. Turbidity high at times, but easily removed. Color slight.(Chief Engineer Gooshine agreed to forward translation of report of the River Experiment Station, not available when we left Moscow).

Elevation of water level at proposed intake about 8 meters lower than Moscow River at Rubleva. Route for pipelines to Moscow along Serpukhovsky Highway and Railway. Site for reserve and regulatory reservoir available about 86 KM from Oka River, and 19 KM from Moscow Ring Railroad, at elevation 87.9 meters. From here flow can be by gravity to the City Pumping Station.

First project figured for 30 million pails per day, for compression with Volga Station. Two pipelines, 1 1/2 meters diameter. 15 million pails each = 48.5 mgd. Each. 1 1/2 meters = 59"

Force main section, 86.1 km long, from River to reserve reservoir. See Profile, Insert 12, Vol. 2 Researches (gray book) =282,000 feet.

60" pipe (6=12c) loss of head = 0.8 per 1000 carrying 48.5 mgd. V= 3.94' per sec. 0.8' x 282 = 225.6 feet total loss. Loss as shown in Profile. Elevation 156.8 meters 87.9= 68.7 meters = 226 feet.

The cost of the project complete for 30 million pails, including the pumping station and filter plant at the Oka River, 2 1.5 meters diameter. Steel pipelines, 119 km long, reserve reservoir, city pumping station, etc., is estimated at 214 million Rubles. Estimate has been made with a number of different pipe line schemes. One using 3 lines, 1.3 meters diameter, of which 59 km would be steel, the remaining 60 km of wood, was estimated to cost 195 million Rubles (See Tom 1, additional Researchers of 1927 & 1928, pages 74 to 79).

In 1928, 29 further studies made, and topography of routes. Part gravity schemes investigated, using reinforced concrete conduit about 2 meters x 2 meters. Project based on 40 million pails per day. See blueprint profiles #6733 and 6734, dated March 26, 1929. Two pump stations proposed in all pumping projects, one at river, the second 30 KM distant to deliver water to reserve and regulatory reservoir 86 KM distant from river. From here gravity flow to reservoir and city pumping station on so called Sokoline Mountain. Total lengths of pipelines to Sokoline Mountain, 115 km with pumping scheme. 125 km with part gravity project. Saving in pumping lift by gravity scheme about 17 meters. Route 10 km longer.

NUMBER 3: MOSCOW RIVER IMPOUNDING RESERVOIR PROJECT

As previously stated, safe yield of unregulated Moscow River, during dry years = 60 million pails per day. Of this 40 million pails required to maintain navigation below Moscow, leaving only 20million pails per day available for water supply. Present consumption rapidly nearing this figure. Project proposes to materially increase the available dry weather flow by the construction of a regulating dam in the river at Rubleva, and 3 large impounding reservoirs on the upper Moscow, and two tributaries, the Estra and Ruza, with a fourth reserve reservoir on the Ozerna. (See sketch No. 1, Tom 2, 1929, page 44, showing layout and catchment areas). Impounded water stored during freshets, will be released as required during dry periods, flowing down present stream channels to regulating dam at Rubleva, from where it will be filtered and pumped to the city as at present, thus dispensing with long pipelines required for Volga and Oka projects.

Regulatory Dam The first step in this project is the regulating dam across the Moscow River at Rubleva. This is now under construction. Large coffer dam for approximately first 2/3 of installation nearing completion. Cylindrical "Roller Lilt" type, German patents, adopted as best for Moscow's severe winter conditions. Provides close regulation of flow. Possibility of ice going on rollers. One center pier. Two shore piers. Two rollers, 3 1/2 meters diameter, approximately 30 meters long, in clear, each. Elevation of water, with dam, raised 3.5 meters above present summer level.
See Tom 2, 1929 Researchers, Page 120, for preliminary sketch of proposed dam.

See Tom 2, 1929 Researchers, Page 141, for location of dam, and sedimentation basins, with reference to Rubleva Station.

See Tom 2, 1929 Researchers, Page 137, for location of dam, and sedimentation basins.

Dam to this height will impound 5 million cubic meters (407.5 million pails = 1320 million gallons). Mass diagram studies of flow in river at Rubleva, during driest recorded years 1921 1922, indicate that with the impounded reserve afforded by the dam, a flow of no less than 9.75 meters per second or 68.5 million pails per day can be guaranteed all year round. Deducting 40 million pails per day required for navigation, leaves 28.5 million pails per day available for water supply purposes. (= 92 mgd) (See Tom 2, 1929 Researches, pages 113 & 114.

With approximately 2.5 million pails available from Mitischensky and Oldenborg wells, a total supply of 31 million pails (100 million gallons) will be possible, upon completion of the dam and extensions to the Rubleva Station and filter plant, which are also under construction.

Filter Plant Extensions

Upon completion of units, now building, filter plant at Rubleva will comprise 7 sedimentation basins, 94 prefilter and 27 slow filter sand filters. New units same size as former units. This will permit filtered output of about 22 million pails per day, operated at same rate as present units.

Following this final extension of the prefilters, slow sand plant will be made to 8 sedimentation basins, 108 pre-filter and 35 slow sand filters. This expected to provide about 28.5 million pails per day, using slow sand filters at present rates, but increasing rate on prefilters, due to improved coagulation with new mixing basin, and improved sedimentation from new plain sedimentation basins at regulatory dam. (See layout plan. Tom 2, page 141)

The department engineer generally considers that when fully extended as proposed, the prefilter slow sand plant will handle about 30 million pails (97 mgd) per day. It would offer that under normal condition this plant could be depended upon for substantially greater output with close attention to chlorination, but limits must be based on a worst condition of excessive turbidities and high bacterial counts, during spring break up, and fall rain.

New Rapid Filter Plant

Preliminary plans are prepared for construction, in successive stages, of a new filter plant, rapid sand type, with estimate capacity of 30 million pails, following completion of final extension to present prefilter slow sand plant. New plant to be located at Rubleva, south of existing filters. The low lift pumping station to be built in near future at the east end of the new sedimentation basins at the regulatory dam, will later on supply the new rapid filter plant with raw water. Two large steel pipelines, about 2 km long, will be laid in the next 2 or 3 years from the new low lift station to the present filter plant, and 2 additional lines will be required later to supply the new rapid filters. Additional high lift pumps to be provided as required.

Estra River Dam & Impounding Reservoir

It is proposed to begin construction this Fall, on the Estra River Dam as the first step in the upper river impounded supplies.

Detailed studies of the average daily water level and flow of the river have been made since 1919. (See Tom 2, pages 145 to 162) at the Measuring Station at Bugarovosky.

Figures and date in report (Tom 2) based on proposed dam 12.8meters high (water depth above present average level), located at Srikavo. Inundated area 95.5 hectares. Catchment area above dam 970 square km. Vol impounded about 40 million cubic meters.
The department engineers estimated that with 40 million cubic meters impounded in Estra Dam, together with the 5 million cubic meters in the dam at Rubleva, a flow of no less than 11.5 cubic meters per second or 80,5 million pails per day, can be guaranteed at Rubleva, during driest years. Deducting 40 million pails for navigation, leaves 40.5 million pails available for water supply purposes from the Moscow River.

Criticism of the shallowness of the proposed reservoir by German engineering specialists Drs. Eiginbrudt and Brulina and engineer Prince, in reports on the project in 1929, has evidently influenced the Department to increase the proposed depth from 12.8 meters to 17 meters of water depth above the present stream level.

An earth dam is proposed, with no core wall. Total length of dam about 450 to 480 meters. 6 feet below elevation of flow line, about 161 meters above sea level.

Country very attractive and location generally satisfactory for impounding reservoir. Inundation will approach forest area which will line edge of reservoir on one side for miles. Studies of geological conditions made at two possible sites. With 17 meters depth, storage capacity will be 110 million cubic meters at upper site; 120 million cubic meters at lower site, or approximately 3 times the storage capacity first proposed with dam 12.8 meters high.

Ratio of storage capacity to average annual flow about 50 to 60%. Rainfall generally averages about 540 m.m.. Runoff about 250 m.m. or 37%.
With catchment area above Estra Dam of 970 square kilometers = 970 million square meters x 20 m.m. runoff = 194 million cubic meters annual run off. Proposed storage of 110 million c.m. divided by 194 = 57% ratio for Estra.

Records for 5 year period 1919 1926, showed average depth of precipitation 525 m.m. runoff 32%. Ratio of proposed storage, using these figures, 60.5%.

Figures of Department not obtained for guaranteed flow at Rubleva with dam at Estra 17 meters high, and increase from 40 to 110 or possibly 120 million cubic meters storage capacity. Mass diagram studies required, and allowance for additional losses due to increased evaporation from greater surface of reservoir, and travel down stream to Rubleva. Length along stream from Estra Dam to Rubleva about 75 KM. 946.5 MILES)

Increase from 40 to 110 million cubic meters stage, may increase amount available for water supply purposes at Rubleva from 40.5 to possibly 55 million pails per day, accepting Department figures for net increase with smaller storage. This consumption will be met in 1938, according to latest estimates for future needs.

Impounding Reservoirs on Ruza and Upper Moscow Rivers

As required the Department proposes to meet the future demands by impounded supplies on the Ruza and Upper Moscow. Both locations have been examined and appear generally satisfactory as reservoir sites. Earth dams are planned.

Water shed area above proposed dam on Ruza = 1150 square km. Water shed area above proposed dam on Moscow = 1430 square km.

First proposed dam 13.4 meters high (water depth above present average level) on Ruza and 12.8 meters on Upper Moscow owing to great shallow area, now propose to increase to 17 18 meters depth. With better depth, Ruza will impound about 130 million cubic meters.
Length of travel down stream from Ruza dam to Rubleva, about 133 km. From dam site on Upper Moscow to Rubleva, about 145 km.

Ozerna Reserve

In addition to the Estra, and Ruza and Upper Moscow developments, the Department also plans, when the need arises, to provide an additional supply, as a reserve, by the construction of a dam on the Ozerna River, a tributary of the Ruza. (See plan TOM 2, page 44), utilizing an existing lake, known as Trostenasky Lake, about 4 km diameter. Propose to raise the level of this lake about 4 meters, and provide total storage of about 200 million cubic meters. The water shed above the dam site is small, about 380 square km, and the reservoir would probably require 3 to 4 years to fill.

Department's Estimates of Total Yield

With storage reservoirs on the Estra, Ruza and Moscow Rivers of 110, 130 and 185 million cubic meters, and 5 million cubic meters at Rubleva dam, total impounded water will aggregate 430 million cubic meters = 35 billion pails = 113 billion gallons, and Department estimates that this storage, exclusive of the Ozerna reserve of 200 million cubic meters (= 16.3 billion pails = 53 billion gallons) will guarantee a flow at Rubleva of no less than 100 million pails (= 324 million gallons) per day, at driest periods.

The latest approved consumption figures call for 93.6 million pails in 1950. (See table page), and if provision is made for the anticipated 4 million population in 1950 within the ring railroad limits, of 250 liters (66 gallons) per capita per day, and for the additional 2 million outside those limits at 100 liters (26 gallons) per capita per day, as stated, the total consumption in 1950 will aggregate 97.8 million pails per day.

It is evident that even with the Ozerna reserve, steps must be taken by 1950 or sooner, to supplement the supply from some other source or by further development of the Moscow River watershed.

The catchment area of the Moscow River and it's tributaries is 7350 square km at Rubleva. Of this total 3930 square KM, or 53.5% will be utilized by the combined catchment area of the Upper Moscow, Estra, Ruza and Ozerna. The Department considers further development possible and has given some study to additional reservoirs on the Iskona, big and little Estra, Ozerna and on the Moscow River between Ruza and Estra Rivers. They have computed that with this ultimate system of storage reservoirs, with volume up to 60% of the average run off from the catchment area, there is the possibility of making available at Rubleva, for water supply purposes, about 2,100,000 cubic meters per day, = to 170 million pails =550 gallons per day.

COMPARISON OF PROJECTS Approximate Cost Figures

Comparative cost figures were first made by the Department, for the various schemes, based on an additional supply of 30 million pails, by 1950. (See Tom 1, Estra Reservoir, Pages 83, 84, 85.)

For this capacity it was figured the total cost of the development, exclusive of the distribution system., would be 195 million rubles; the Volga 185 million rubles, and the Moscow impounding reservoir scheme, only 107 million rubles.

Operating costs, per 1000 square meters of water supplied, figured at 197 rubles for Oka (with steel pipelines); 213 Rubles for Volga; and 124 Rubles for Moscow. Present cost of supplying water, 153 Rubles per 1,000 cubic meters. (= 15.3 Kopeks per cubic meter = 40.298 per 1,000 gallons).

Unit costs high. Include interest and sinking fund charges at 7.82%, also operating and interest costs on capital item of 33 million Rubles for extension to distribution system.
Following recent expansion of policy and decision that normal plant capacity of at least 90 million pails per day, (100 million pails maximum) would be required by 1950, of which 30 million would be supplied by the present Rubleva plant, and 60 million from new work, the Department estimated that the total cost of such work with the impounding reservoir scheme, including new regulating dam (exc. of the two settling reservoirs along the river), extensions to the present Rubleva filter plant and station to 30 million pails capacity, construction of the new 30 million pail rapid filter plant and pumping station, construction of a future 30 million pail filter plant and pumping station, dams and impounding reservoirs on Estra, Ruza, and Upper Moscow and Ozerna , etc., all plants to aggregate 90 million pails capacity per day, with ability to provide 12% additional for maximum daily needs, or about 100 million pails per day, maximum demand, all for a total of 159.4 million Rubles.

It was estimated that corresponding facilities, with the additional 60 million pails obtained from the Oka River , with the required long pipelines, would total 268 million Rubles for the all funding scheme with steel pipes, and 296 million with part steel pumping lines and part concrete gravity conduits.

Ultimate costs of serving, upon final development, was estimated at 10 Kopeks per square meter with the Moscow impounding reservoir project, and 17 Kopeks per square meter, with the Oka supply. (= 19.5 and 33.1 cents per 1,000 gallons, respectively).

Department Approval of Moscow River Source

The question of selection of the new source is a most serious one, confronting the Department Engineers, and studies of all projects have been made in great detail, as evidenced by the voluminous reports, and experimental plant work on the Oka and Volga Rivers at the preferred sites. The engineers are to be commended in the highest terms on the thoroughness and completeness of these studies.

Consideration of the Volga as the future source was practically eliminated, following the experimental plant work, particularly due to the high color at times of low water periods, previously referred to, and the necessary high operating cost for satisfactory treatment.

Department approval is now apparently given to the Moscow River Impounding Reservoir Project, in preference to the Oka River, principally from the standpoint of it's relative cheapness in construction and operation, and the first steps of the development are now under construction.

The water supply problems and selection of the future source have been the subject of many published articles in the public press and much public discussion by various engineers and others (See Tom 1, Researches 1927 1928.)

An article by Mr. N. L. Gooschine, Chief Engineer of the Water Works, on page 38 is of interest. He states that (not literal translation) "The basic and most complete solution of the water supply of Moscow, is a supply from the Oka or Volga Rivers. These sources are nonexhausting and will satisfy the demands for an indefinite time. If financial conditions will permit, then this plan will be the best to carry out. But financial difficulties and some technical considerations make us prefer the impounding reservoir scheme, which will only cost 1/2 as much as the Oka supply.

"It is quite enough that the Impounding Reservoir Scheme will supply Moscow for 25 years, and all bonds retired. In all cities financial difficulties are paramount, and makes people prefer the cheapest schemes, which are not always the best. The drawback to the Reservoir Scheme may be as to quality. Unfortunate conditions may be obviated by careful technical construction of the impounding reservoirs and correct purification and disinfection of the water. The problem is so conflicted that Moscow cannot make the decision by itself."

Mr. Gooschine also referred to improved flow conditions in the Moscow River which might be expected following the development by impounding reservoir, and the significance for improved navigation and fighting floods. On page 12, in the same report, Professor S. N. Stroganov, eminent scientist in charge of all sewage treatment investigations, and consulted for the Water Trust, stated, among other things, that (not literal translation):

"The water supply is of the greatest importance for big city, and must look decades ahead. The Oka and Volga are great rivers, with large catchment areas, nearly equal. In both rivers the quality is good enough for water supply purposes, and the quantity stable. Of impounding reservoirs on the River Moscow, we are dealing with structures which can change the quality of the water. In Russia we have no experience with impounding supplies, and may make a problem with many unknown elements. The question is simpler and clearer with supplies from the Oka or Volga."

Professor Stroganov further refers to the comparative qualities of the Oka and Volga waters the Oka with higher hardness, etc., the Volga with higher organic matter and high color. States that low bacterial counts in both rivers are favorable; that there is greater self purification in the Oka.

He refers to the present and possible sources of pollution of the impounding reservoir supplies, which would be helped by making a sanitary zone, and the reservoir will be in places of considerable population, with a few hills, great length and small depth, with possibilities of great quantity of plankton. He discusses the possibility of changing of lake plankton in the flow down the river. He concluded with an interesting statement that "A source of water supply from the Moscow River, making no more than two impounding reservoirs, and with ultimate development to four of them, is as safe as the Volga or Oka, and economic financial consideration must control in selection."

Population Control on Watersheds

The existing population on the Moscow River and it's tributaries above Rubleva, is quite substantial, and is rapidly increasing. The population in a 700 km radius from Rubleva, increased from 116,000 to 177,000, or 55% since 1920 and within a 25 km radius increased from 15,600 in 1915 to 30,000 in 1926. Near Rubleva, several large estates, formerly occupied by a few wealthy families, have become rest homes, where hundreds of people live. There are also five or six large summer health resorts, with a large summer population.

In July 1922, in order to more adequately guard the water supply, the Board of Moscow Soviet broadened the scope of the sanitary zone established in 1915, to cover an area of about 200 square km, almost 1/3 of the Moscow River watershed above Rubleva, on which about 520 populated places are located, including 3 factories,12 hospitals, 9 sanitariums, 8 children's homes, etc. The duties of the officials in charge of the sanitary zone are watching water borne infection, sanitary improvement of villages, factories and other institutions, establishment of water supplies, and sewer treatment plants, etc.

Another possible source of serious pollution above Rubleva, is the sand and gravel industry in which hundreds of people are engaged. This dredging is carried out in both summer and winter.

In the construction of the impounding reservoirs on the Estra, Ruza and Upper Moscow, many roads, homes and other buildings will be submerged, requiring substantial sums for removal, relocation, or other damages. The approximate population adjacent to the shores of the reservoirs, when completed is stated to be about 6600 on the Estra, 3100 on Ruza, and 6900 on Upper Moscow.
It is planned to establish a central protective zone within the Sanitary Zone, for a length of 25 km, and a width of 1 km on each bank of the river and it's tributaries. Inside the limits of three zones, severe sanitary measures are to be Within the first two months, a proclamation has been issued by the Commission of Moscow Soviet, on taking extraordinary measures in guarding the water supply zone. The proclamation is in the form of a large poster with a map showing the districts of severe sanitary guard, the forbidden districts for taking gravel and sand, picnics excursions, etc., the districts in which, in addition to the above, it is forbidden to bathe or pasture cattle, and the districts in which villages must be removed. The villages in which the order is enforced are listed. The first group comprises villages situated on both banks of the Moscow River and tributaries, within stretches 1 km wide and 25 km long, above Rubleva Station, and include 24 villages on the Moscow, 4 on the Estra, and 21 on other tributaries. The second group comprises other villages situated in a narrow zone outside the first zone, and include 18 on the Estra and 9 more on the Moscow, making a total of 76 villages affected by the order. Penalty of 3000 Rubles fine or 3 years imprisonment are prescribed for violation.

Reports by German Specialists

In June 1928, studies and reports on the various projects were made by German expert, Dr. Eigenbrott and Engineer Prince, of Simens Baurminion, and by Professor Dr. Bruns of the Institute of Hygiene and Bacteriology. The Engineers approved of the construction of the regulating dam in the Moscow River at Rubleva, with a suggestion that it be built with 3 times the proposed capacity of 5 million cubic meters, but expressed the view that increase of pumping from the Moscow River was a temporary measure, and in future, works will be transported to the Oka River.

Dr. Bruns discussed the small flow of the Moscow River and expressed the view that even with four impounding reservoirs it would only serve for a few years. He referred to the shallowness of the proposed reservoir, the probability of bad tastes and odors from algae matters, the large population on the watershed, and great contamination, etc., and stated that from the standpoint of hygiene, the Moscow Impounded supply can only be approved if no other source is available.
He stated that water from the Volga, owing to it's unfavorable qualities (high color) also on account of the navigation reservoirs, cannot be given serious consideration.

He concluded that the plan of a filtered water supply rom the Oka is best, and that if obtained from the Volga or Moscow, it would require complicated methods of purification.

CONCLUSIONS AND RECOMMENDATIONS

Choice of Project: The Moscow River, developed by impounding reservoirs, or the Oka River.

A satisfactory quality of filtered water is now being furnished from the Moscow River at Rubleva, during normal periods of flow. Difficult to handle during high turbidity periods of spring breakup and fall rain. Improvement of facilities for sedimentation and coagulation should lessen difficulties.

Continuance of this source, and further development may be satisfactory for a period of years, but may be extremely hazardous to place full dependence upon it for future water supply of greater Moscow.

Project commends itself particularly on account of cheapness, as compared with the Oka Project, and less initial outlay in gradual development. The estimates of the Department for the costs of both projects would be an interesting subject for review, giving consideration to the possible economy of large steel pipelines for the Oka Project, laid in accordance with modern American practice.

A supply from the Oka River is far less involved than development of the Moscow. The river at the proposed site for the intake, pumping station, and filter plant is about 5 times as large as the Moscow River and is in many ways an ideal source of supply for a great city. With an average flow of about 1050 and a minimum flow of about 300 pails per day, it provides an adequate supply, without regulation to serve the city for an indefinite period. It is broad and deep at the site, and the water is of high quality, low in turbidity and bacteria, and easy to treat. Full knowledge of treatment required is available through operation of the large resting station for a period over a year. The population above the site is small, and prospects of substantial increases in population is remote. The river has great power of self purification, and oxidation of organic polluting matters from farm run off and the small contributory population.

The development of a supply from the Oka occasioned no especially complicated engineering or sanitary procedure. An intake structure, pumping station with low and high lift pumps, rapid filter plant and clear well, two pipelines to the city of large diameter, and one or more receiving reservoirs of large capacity as a reserve for city distribution. The cost of such a reservoir should not be chargeable against the Oka project, as the reservoir capacity of the present system is altogether inadequate and additional capacity must be provided in any event. The problem of supply from the Oka is clear cut and definitive, with the assurance that upon it's delivery, the city will be provided with a water of surpassing quality, and from a practically inexhaustible source. Railroad and highway facilities to the site and lines are good.

The supply from the Moscow, on the other hand, presents many unknown factors, from the standpoint of quantity, quality, taste and odor, regulation, sanitation, supervision and control, possible interference with future increase in navigation, curtailing of development of a great area in close proximity to Moscow, etc.

The proposed suggested development of the entire water shed above Rubleva, as outlined under the heading "Department Estimates of Total Yield" to provide 170 million pails per day for water supply purposes, is questionable for an area in such close proximity to the city. The three proposed reservoirs on the Estra, Ruza, and Upper Moscow, according to the Department's figures, as previously stated, will make available 100 million pails at Rubleva, with the large storage on the small Ozerna watershed used as a reserve. These developments utilize 53% of the total watershed area above Rubleva. Further development to the extent of 100% of the watershed area above Rubleva it is believed, would not be in the best interests of the future city. The proposed limits of the city itself in 1950, with a diameter of 30 miles, will encroach on this territory. With a population of 6 million within the 1950 city limits, the suburban population, beyond these limits, and the city will be confronted with an ever increasing burden of supervision and restriction to maintain practically it's sole source of water supply, in satisfactory sanitary condition. The complete tying up of this great area of 7350 square kilometers, or 2840 square miles, under complete watershed development, may seriously affect the future growth and expansion of the city. It would seem that the development propose4d with the four projected reservoirs is the reasonable limit beyond which it would be inadvisable to go, (see conclusions of Professor Stroganoff, page) and if this development is carried out, making available 100 million pails per day, at Rubleva, the city is definitely and forever committed to the problem of maintaining safe and satisfactory sanitary conditions in the watershed tributaries and the river itself, with it's sole supply drawn from a point in the river within the limits of a great and growing city. Already, the somewhat drastic order of the Moscow Government, affecting 76 villages within the present sanitary protective zone above Rubleva seriously curtails the farming, industrial and recreational and other activities of the inhabitants, and it is understood has aroused much unfavorable public sentiment. Whenever possible, sources of water supply more remote from a great city are looked upon with more favor and confidence by the public. It is unquestionable that public opinion would give preference to the remote Oka supply rather than to further extensions of the nearby Moscow watershed, with it's attendant restrictions. The recreational needs of a great city of 6 million people are a matter for severe consideration. The Moscow River and it's tributaries above the city form the logical playground for such activities, which will become accessible to the public in a few years when automobiles come into more general use.

Assuming that the development of the Moscow River watershed will terminate with the 4 reservoirs as projected, the question now arises, will this development, making approximately 100 million pails available for water supply purposes and allowing 40 million pails for navigation, serve the city until 1950.

The Department estimates, as referred to on page 21, call for a 93.6 million pails by 1950, to provide for a population of 4 million within the present city ring railway limits, and 2 million in the new outer zone. If, as stated, a per capita allowance 250 liters (66 gallons) per day is made for the 4 million in the inner city, and 100 liters (26 gallons) outside, the 1950 requirements will be 97.8 million pails per day, thus almost equalizing the limit of supply by the 4 reservoir development, and making additional facilities necessary. With this total, the average consumption for the whole city of 6 million, will be 53 gallons per capita per day.

This rate of consumption is almost double the present rate. It is, in general in line with present European practice, but substantially lower than American practice for large cities, which show per capita consumption rates ranging from about 75 gallons to as high as 275 gallons per day. Instance of average water consumption of 75 gallons per capita or less are rare, even for 100% metered cities.

With the consumption of the colossal countryside industrial development under the 5 year plan, and the subsequent activities, it is anticipated that Moscow, as the capital and largest city of the Soviet Republic, will rank with the world's greatest cities, in industry and modern city progress. A secondary position, it is understood, is not the aim of the present government. If this outstanding position is attained, one of the most important contributing factors will be the education of it's citizens to a liberal use of water by the general introduction of modern plumbing, and ample allowance for industrial, commercial and other public use. With such provisions, corresponding to present general American practices, it is a matter for serious consideration whether or not the proposed consumption of 53 gallons per capita will not be exceeded by 1950.

In regard to future navigation, no especial study has been given to this phase of the problem. The river is navigable below Moscow, forming part of the Oka Volga navigation system. Steamer service connects Moscow with Nigni Novgorod. A minimum flow of 40 million pails per day is deemed essential for present navigation requirements. In a general way, it would seem possible that with the future great industrial requirement of the city, the need might arise for improved navigation facilities, with boats of greater draft requiring a deeper flow in excess of the present 40 million pails as the minimum.

Some questions also arise as to the possible quality of water drawn from the proposed impounding reservoirs. Following the criticism of shallowness by the German specialists the plans were revised to provide greater depth, from about 13 to 17 meters. Even with this depth in the stream beds, vast areas of the submerged lands will be very shallow. Under these conditions difficulties will inevitably arise from algae growth, with probability of objectionable tastes and odors, and possible interference with filtration. Such troubles will undoubtedly be lessened by the long travel downstream to Rubleva, but these conditions give rise to an element of uncertainty.

It is believed to be self evident that with the future supply drawn from the improved Moscow River at Rubleva, the most careful supervision and control will be mandatory, at all times of the reservoirs, streams, filter plant and entire 2800 square miles of watershed. The operating personnel for such a system will necessarily be greater than with a supply from Oka River. It would seem quite possible that the apparent advantage of the cheaper Moscow River project would very likely be more than offset long before 1950, in the losses sustained by restrictions imposed by the plan, interference with city and suburban development, and greater future operating costs than are at present anticipated. Furthermore the practical limit of the impounded Moscow supply it is believed will be reached by 1950, making necessary the development of a supply from the Oka River by that time or sooner.

The writer spent six weeks in Moscow. Part OFB this time was spent on the problems of sewage treatment. About two weeks was occupied by plant and site inspection. It is felt that the time devoted to study of the general water situation was entirely too short to become familiar with all details of the involved problem, which has been the subject of studies and planning by the Water Department Engineer for the past 15 years or more. Unfamiliarity with the Russian language made the accumulation and assembly of data more difficult.

The selection of the best source of supply and the development of the same with plant and equipment conforming to the modern practice and ideals of present day water works, is a problem of the utmost importance for the future city of Greater Moscow. In the light of all the facts and information at hand. I am of the opinion that the best interests of the future city of Greater Moscow will be served by the early construction of the Oka River project. I can readily appreciate however, that scant consideration may be given to a recommendation calling for such a radical change of the adopted program based as it is on such brief study. The desire has been expressed by the Moscow Government officials, for a more complete study of the water situation by a commission of American Engineers, working under or in conjunction with the most eminent authority in American water work practice. The importance of the problem unquestionably justifies such action.

Respectfully submitted,

Isaac Stanley Walker
Consulting Engineer
850 Drexel Building
Philadelphia, Pennsylvania

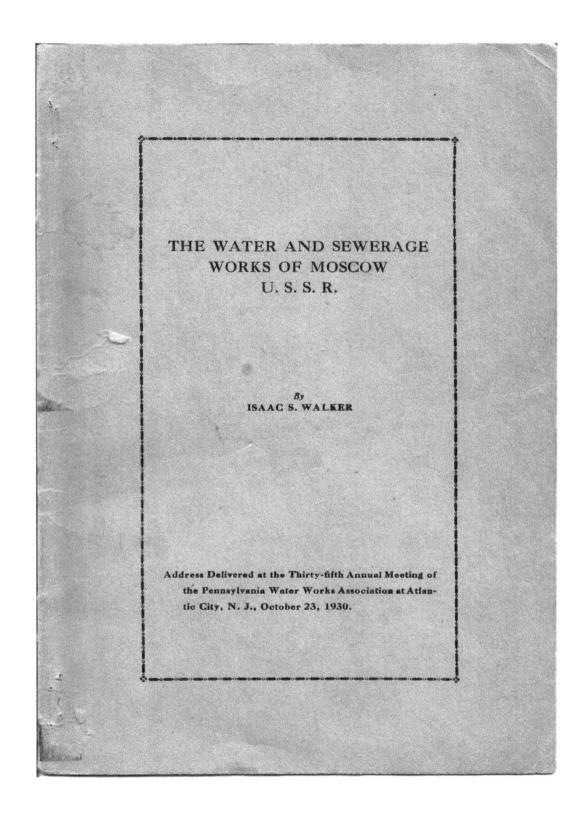

THE WATER AND SEWERAGE
WORKS OF MOSCOW
U. S. S. R.

By
ISAAC S. WALKER

**Address Delivered at the Thirty-fifth Annual Meeting of
the Pennsylvania Water Works Association at Atlantic City, N. J., October 23, 1930.**

THE WATER AND SEWERAGE WORKS OF MOSCOW, U. S. S. R.

By Isaac S. Walker

About the middle of May it was the privilege of the writer to visit Moscow, to make a study of and report on projects for additional water supply and sewerage works for the City, as now contemplated by the Russian Government. Needless to say, in view of the many conflicting stories we hear of Russian activities, it was the most interesting and illuminating experience in my career, to date.

Immediately following my arrival in Moscow, on May 31st, my first three weeks were spent in an intensive program of inspections of existing works, proposed new sites and in numerous conferences with engineers and officials. The water and sewerage works are under the direction of the so-called "Water and Canalazation Trust," headed by a commissioner or Commissar. In both departments I was impressed with the technical skill of the designing and supervising engineers and chemists and with the exhaustive study given to the comprehensive plans for both water and sewerage works. I found an exceptionally complete set of studies, reports and records, covering the proposed extensions, as well as contour maps, plans, descriptions, meteorological records and other necessary engineering and analytical data on existing works.

The study of the water and sewerage problems for a city of two and one-half million people is no light problem at best, but here the difficulties were multiplied owing to my ignorance of the language and the necessity of acquiring all information through an interpreter. Hundreds of girls are acting in this capacity but I was assigned a young man of 19 years, who had some experience in the technical work of the department, and I cannot compliment this boy too highly. Never outside of Russia, he spoke five languages fluently. His ability in interpretation was remarkable, which was of great help in the investigation and translation work.

Moscow, as you know, is the capital and largest city of the Soviet Republics. It lies near the center of the East European Plain, about 56 degrees N. Latitude and 37½ degrees E. Longitude, on the Moscow River. It is the greatest city of industry and trade. Eleven railroads radiate from Moscow to all sections of the Union.

The average yearly temperature is about 50 degrees F. The winters are very severe, lasting about five months, but the summers are hot. Rainfall records covering the last 35 years, are available, showing an average of about 21 inches at Moscow.

The population in 1929, according to Water Department figures, was almost two and one-half millions. An increase to four millions is anticipated by 1950, within the present limits, which cover about 81 sq. miles of territory. It is expected, however, that due to further expansion beyond present limits, Greater Moscow, in 1950, will have a population of six millions, and plans for future water and sewerage works are being projected on this basis.

The city, which dates from about the year 1150, has grown in a series of concentric zones around the Kremlin, the inner walled city, with encircling ring streets and boulevards and a ring railway at the limits of the present outer zone. The surface of the city is moderately hilly, with elevations above mean sea level ranging from 400 to 550 feet.

The first public water supply for the city was built about 150 years ago, during the reign of Catherine the Great. The water from some large springs about 10 or 12 miles from the city was collected and conveyed in a brick aqueduct, across the valley of the Ruza River, to a distributing point in the city. This served for almost 50 years, or until about 1825, when the aqueduct broke, following which a pumping station was built, and the first cast iron pipes were laid to carry the water to a tower in the city, which supplied the head for a number of distributing fountains. The old tower is still standing, and in use as a museum.

This system served until about 1860, when a well system was constructed at Mitishensky, another pumping station built, and about 30 miles of C. I. distribution pipes were laid. At this time, however, there was no water in the houses, and the total supply only about 2 mgd.

During the next 40 years, the well system was further developed and two imposing pressure towers were built in the city, but Moscow was far behind other large European cities in water supply facilities. Even in 1900 the total public supply was only about 4 mgd, for a population at that time of about one million.

About 1898, however, a sewer system was constructed and comprehensive plans made for a new water supply. As the available yield from the wells was inadequate, the engineers turned to the Moscow River.

The river has its source about 110 miles west of Moscow, and flows into the Oka River about 80 miles southeast of the city. Due to its winding course, however, it has a total length of about 300 miles. The watershed, above the water works intake, is about 2,840 sq. miles. At Moscow the river has a width of 175 to 200 feet. Below the city the river is navigable, forming a branch of the Volga River Navigation System. There is a substantial population on the watershed, and as the river also carries high turbidity at times, especially during the ice break-up in April, careful filtration is necessary.

The first installment of the filtration system was completed about 1903 and comprised an elaborate intake structure, pumping station, sedimentation basins, slow sand filters, filtered water and distributing reservoirs. The latter is located on an elevation in the city, known as Variobesky Hill. The filter plant is located near the village of Rubleva, about 30 miles above the city center measured along the winding river, but only about 10 miles by air line.

Additions to the filter plant have been made from time to time, and the system improved by the installation of preliminary filters, coagulation and chlorination facilities. As it now stands, the filtration system of Moscow is quite similar to the present double filtration system of Philadelphia, and comprises two large pumping station structures, high and low duty pumps, operated by steam, Diesel engines and electric motors, six large sedimentation basins with 10 hour retention period, 80 pre-filters, operated at a rate of about 40 million gallons per acre per day, 22 slow sand filters, 3-4 acre each, operated at a rate of about four million gallons per acre per day. The pre-filters are not equipped with operating tables and hydraulic valves, such as we provide in our modern plants, but efficient controllers are provided, both for the pre and final filters.

The total output of the filter plant at the present time, is about 60 million gallons per day. The well system, which has been recently modernized with electric pumps, furnishes about seven millions, making a total for both systems of about 67 mgd.

I was particularly impressed by the skilled technical control and supervision of all departments of the water works and with the measures taken for protection of the supply. All plants are enclosed and under strict guard, and no outsiders are admitted except by pass. So-called sanitary protective zones have been established, both for the river and well supplies. Above the Rubleva intake there are several towns of substantial size, also many small vil-

lages and a number of factories, sanatoriums, rest homes,
etc., which constitute a menace to the supply, and in order
to protect the river and its tributaries from sources of
pollution, a sanitary protective zone was established as
early as 1915. This zone extends for a length of 80 kilometers above the intake and covers an area of 2,000 sq.
kilometers. The officials in charge of the zone are respon-
sible for the general sanitation and improvement of the
villages, factories and other institutions, the establishment
of water supplies and sewage treatment plants, investigation of water-born infections, etc. In some sections of the
zone the most extraordinary and drastic regulations are in
effect, forbidding picnics, excursions, bathing, pasturing of
cattle, etc. In addition it is planned to remove many of
the villages in these forbidden areas. Such procedures are
apparently easy of accomplishment under Soviet rule, and
their pollution problems are simple of solution, in comparison with ours.

The general control of water supply and sources is
under a commission, known as the "Commission for Control of Drinking Water and Sources of City Water Supply,"
which name is generally shortened to "Filtration Commission." The personnel of the commission comprises the important staff of the Department of Water Supply, the man-
agers of the water and sewage laboratories, the biologist
in charge of the filter plant, the manager of the sewage
department, a representative of the sanitary and epidemic
section of the Moscow Health Department, Sanitary Phy-
sicians of the Supply and Protective Zones, a representative
of the Sanitary Institute, and other invited specialists. In
addition to general operation, the Commission has general
control of all filtration construction and comprehensive
planning of extensions to existing structures, ways and
means to improve the quality of the supply, control of the
sanitary protective zones, etc.

The plants are operated under strict laboratory control.

The laboratories are well equipped for routine procedure and research work. Practically all the laboratory workers are women, especially trained for the work. Daily analyses are made of the raw, settled, pre-filtered, final filtered and chlorinated effluents. Complete chemical analyses are made at regular intervals, also analyses of samples from the distribution system. Residual chlorine tests are made every two hours of the water entering and leaving the filtered water basin.

Considering the vague ideas I had of Russia prior to my visit, I must say that some of these unformed impressions underwent a radical change after inspection of the water and sewage works, and contacts with the engineers, chemists and operators in charge. I was, to say the least, a little bit surprised to find works of such high class character, remarkably well operated, producing a water supply of limited quantity, but of superior quality and of which any city might be proud, and to brush shoulders with men of the highest scientific skill and technique in the fields of water supply and sewage treatment.

The personnel of the water department numbers about 900. In addition to the head officials, I was impressed with the calibre of the plant superintendents, foremen and mechanics. On five or six occasions during our visits to different plants, the operator in charge was called upon to give a lecture outlining his plant and its operation, prior to our inspection. In all cases this was done by the operator in a creditable manner, showing a thorough knowledge of his subject. All the plant workmen I saw were apparently on their toes, and keenly interested in their work.

The plants looked well from the standpoint of appearance and general upkeep. They give consideration to making a good impression on visitors, for at the filtered water basin, and also in the distribution reservoir, inspection wells have been arranged to show off the filtered water to advantage. The wells are lined with white tile and an excellent lighting effect provided, by means of green glass in some of the windows. They propose to install submerged electric flare lights in both wells.

All plants are well equipped with work and repair shops. The main repair shop is located at the Mitischensky pumping station, and is particularly well equipped with about 60 different machines, mostly of German make. All machine tool and die work is standardized. The meter repair shop is also well equipped with modern testing and repair apparatus, including several multiple test benches. All services in Moscow are metered, and have been for many years. Large meters of 1½ inch diameter and over are purchased in Germany, but the smaller sizes, also of the Siemens & Halske German velocity type, are manufactured in Moscow and Kiev.

One of the most outstanding items in plant statistics, is that with a population of about two and one-half millions, of which about 1,800,000 receive water in their homes, there are only about 16,000 meters in service. In fact the total number of separate services listed is only about 12,000. This is accounted for by the fact that individual homes of the type we are accustomed to are very infrequent in Moscow. The city is greatly overcrowded, and the people live generally in apartments, flats, tenements, or otherwise in a few rooms in grouped buildings. One listed service, therefore may supply a group of such buildings, or a holding as it is called, in which possibly two or three hundred families may be housed. All service lines are laid not less than seven feet deep and street mains 10 feet deep, on account of deep frost penetration.

Distribution pipes are all cast iron of Russian manufacture, laid with lead joints, and aggregate about 500 miles in the entire system. About 55% of the total city area is piped. Pressures vary from about 30 to 100 pounds per sq. inch. Gate valves are generally of the Ludlow type, and are all installed in brick manholes. I looked in vain for fire hydrants on my arrival in the city, but found they have about 5,300 in the system, located in manholes near street intersections. Portable hydrants with hose outlets are carried by the fire and street departments, and clamped or bolted to the riser in the manhole for use.

All water is sold in Moscow by meter registration, at a fixed rate to workers of 13 Kopecs per 100 pails, equivalent to about 20 cents per 1,000 gallons. Private industries, however, must pay substantially higher rates.

As I stated previously, the present population of the city is nearly two and one-half millions, of which about 1,-800,000 are receiving water in their homes. In addition about 390,000 are served by street hydrants for common use, similar to the old street pump. Considering the entire population the per capita consumption is equivalent to about 26 gallons per day, a very low figure in comparison with our cities.

With the city growing rapidly, and increasing demand due to the industrial and general development, an immediate need for an additional supply is imperative. In supplying this need, and providing for an estimated population of six million by 1950, the engineers are confronted with some very interesting problems. The project calls for an increase in the available supply by 1950, up to 300 mgd., equivalent to 50 gallons per capita. The 1950 population estimated at four millions within the present city limits, however, will be furnished with about 66 gallons per capita, and the two millions in the new outer suburban zone, about 26 gallons per capita. These figures, while much lower than our American practice, are somewhat higher than present general European practice.

The problems of the future supply have been carefully studied for a number of years, and several different projects have been investigated in great detail, and lengthy reports prepared thereon. My time will not permit me to dwell at length on these interesting studies, on which volumes have been written, but briefly the situation is about as follows:

Three principal sources are available; the Volga River which is about 70 miles north of the city; the Oka, about 70 miles south, and the Moscow River, the present main source. The Volga and Oka are both large rivers, with minimum flows about five times as large as the Moscow River and each sufficient to supply the city. At the sites investigated both rivers are of excellent quality, comparatively free from pollution. The water normally is clear, but becomes turbid at times, and filtration is necessary. The river levels are approximately the same as the Moscow River at the city, and pumping is required. The necessary ∙ng pipe lines to the city make the project very expensive. ∙ arge sized experimental rapid sand filter plants have been maintained at both rivers for a period of years, and the department is well posted on the necessary methods of treatment. Of the two, the Oka is preferred, as the water of the Volga becomes highly colored during drought periods, increasing the expense of treatment. The Oka is free from color and a generally excellent source of supply.

The minimum flow of the Moscow River at the present intake is about 195 mgd. Of this amount, however, about 130 mgd. must be permitted to pass the intake in order to maintain navigation below the city, thus leaving only 65 mgd. available for waterworks purposes. The limit is now about reached with the present plant, necessitating immediate steps for an additional supply.

Owing to the great initial expense involved in bringing in supplies from the Oka or Volga, the department has made exhaustive studies, and is now proceeding with a plan to increase the minimum available yield of the Moscow River from 65 mgd. as at present to 300 mgd. in 1950, by means of regulation and impounding reservoirs on the upper reaches of the river and its tributaries, the Ruza, Estra and Ozerne Rivers.

The first step, now under construction, is a roller lift regulating dam across the Moscow River, just above the present intake, with two steel rollers approximately 100 feet long and 12 feet in diameter. This type of dam is selected owing to ice conditions during the spring break-up. This dam, it is calculated will permit taking about 90 mgd. at the intake. The present double filtration plant is now being extended to handle this quantity. Following this, all future filter plants will be of American rapid sand type.

As required, great impounding reservoirs will be constructed, first on the Estra River, then on the upper Moscow and the other tributaries, storing the water during the flood periods, and releasing it during low flows, to run down the stream channels to the present filter plant site.

The thoroughness of the studies in connection with this project, reflect great credit on the department engineers. It is a most interesting study in water conservation. The plan lends itself to gradual extensions as required, and the ultimate construction costs are figured to be only about 60% of the Oka pipe line project, and substantially less operating costs. Unfortunately the requirements for the greater city, by 1950, will exhaust this supply, unless extreme development of the watershed is resorted to, and steps must be taken prior to that time, to secure a new supply from the Oka River. It further commits the city to a nearby source, practically within city limits, and with the involved sanitation and pollution problems of a thickly settled territory.

The related subjects of sewage and sewerage treatment as projected in Moscow are also of great interest, but as my time is limited I will just give you a brief outline of the general situation.

The prinicpal works comprise a separate sewer system, pumping station, extensive sand filtration fields at Lublino and Lubertzy, and the new Koguhovsky aeration plant.

The first installation of the sewer system, and the treatment work at Lublino, was begun in 1893 and completed in 1898. At the present time there are about 380 miles of sewers in the city, generally of tile and brick. Connections to sewers are obligatory.

The main sewage pumping station has been operating since 1898. It is well equipped with modern centrifugal pumps, operated by Diesel engines and electric motors. About three-fourths of all the sewage of the city requires pumping. The sewage is far more concentrated than American sewages. The total volume handled amounts to about 70% of the water supply. One rather unusual feature is the screening arrangement ahead of the pumps, consisting of a series of vertical bar screens spaced about one inch in the clear, with a motor operated cleaning device, discharging on a belt conveyor, which carries the sewage to a grinder. The ground up matters fall back into the inlet channel to be rescreened, the process simply preparing the sewage for passage through the pumps, all matters other than large objects passing to the treatment works.

From the pumping station, the sewage may be pumped to anyone of the three treatment plants. At the present time about 90% of the total is handled at the two filtration fields at Lublino, located about nine miles southeast of the city, and at Lubertzy, which lies about 12.5 miles east. The fields cover vast areas, about 4,300 acres, or almost seven sq. miles being under irrigation. Large additional areas are available for extensions. The soil is sand formation, and the beds are of sand, with underdrains discharging into the main drainage channels, thence to the river.

The filtered effluent from the newer Lubertzy plant, built in 1912, is excellent. Portions of the first Lublino plant have been in use for over 30 years and the capacity of the filter beds is decreased. At the present time this plant is seriously overloaded. Only part of the sewage at these plants is settled prior to discharge on the sand areas, but additional settling tanks together with separate sludge digestion tanks and sludge beds are planned. At the Lublino plant about one million gallons per day is treated by sedimentation and contact filters. Here also is located an experimental biological station, built over 30 years ago, which regularly treats about 300,000 gallons per day. I believe this was one of the earliest sewage experimental plants in Europe.

The latest plant is the Koguhovsky Aeration Station, located on the Moscow River, about six miles south of the city center and put in operation about one year ago. It is a complete activated sludge plant, comprising a machinery and administration building, screens, screenings incinerator, primary and secondary settling tanks, degreasing compartment, aerating and re-aerating tanks, aerating trickling filters, sludge beds, a large fish pond and chlorine disinfection.

Prior to building, experimental work was carried on at the Lublino Experiment Station. The present plant includes some novel construction features and is treating about 3½ mgd. Extensions are being made to increase the capacity to 10 mgd. and will include separate sludge digestion tanks, equipped to utilize the digestion gases for heating the sludge chambers. One of the outstanding features is the aerating trickling filter, of which there are 12 in the present plant, on which the sewage from the secondary settling tanks is sprinkled in the usual manner, controlled by Miller siphons. The filters are of slag, four meters deep, placed in concrete boxes, with an air chamber underneath. With the forced air method, these filters are operated at a rate of 8 to 10 times the customary rates for strong European sewage. The plant is producing an effluent of exceptionally high quality.

The expense of additional sewerage and sewage treatment works for Greater Moscow will run into large figures and the problems have been approached in a business like manner, with a carefully studied comprehensive plan, setting forth proposed extensions of main sewers and treatment works for each five year period, to 1950. The Russian engineers approach problems with great care and consideration on matters of such magnitude. The Koguhovsky Activated Sludge Plant, while it will assist in relieving the present immediate need for additional treatment facilities, is considered more or less as an experimental station, the aim of which is to obtain actual working data showing the technical and economic value of such intensive treatment, as compared with the older methods.

Judging from the hundreds of questions which have been asked me since my return from Russia, it appears very few people here have any conception of the country or its people. To many, I believe, this brief outline of the activities of the Russian Government in their water and sewerage work may be somewhat of a revelation. This paper is not the place for a discussion of general conditions, and not being a profound student of world economics, I do not consider myself qualified to pass judgment on, or forecast the outcome of what is frequently referred to as the greatest experiment in government in the world's history. I may say, however, that the entire country, or at least what I saw of it in Moscow and vicinity, is a bee-hive of energy. Everyone appears to be working, with an aim in view, and unemployment is apparently not a problem in Russia. All endeavors appear to be directed toward the consummation of the five year plan, which, in its general scope, is said to be the most outstanding and comprehensive program ever inaugurated by any nation, calling for the expenditure of some 39 billions of dollars for economic reconstruction of the country within that period. As to the ultimate outcome, I can only say, judging from my own limited observations, that if all other activities of reconstruction, development and governmental functions are carried forward with the same degree of intelligence, skill and technical administration, as is evidenced in the water and sewerage works of Moscow, there is some hope of a bright day dawning for the Russian people.

Discussion Following the Address Delivered at the Thirty-fifth Annual Meeting of the Pennsylvania Water Works Association at Atlantic City, N.J.
October 23, 1930 by Isaac S. Walker

The Water and Sewerage Works of Moscow

Mr. Chester. Cannot Mr. Walker stay on the platform and let us ask him some questions, Mr. President?

The President. I think Mr. Walker would be perfectly willing to answer any question you may have to ask him.

Mr. Walker. Certainly.

Mr. Chester. John Ledoux wants us to first ask you why you did not select a girl as interpreter, instead of a boy?

Mr. Walker. Mr. Ledoux would think that. We probably know that some of the Russian girls are easy on the eyes, and wants me to admit my sad error.

Mr. Chester. With regard to the sewage disposal, they screened out the coarse stuff and then ground it up, so as to get it through the pumps?

Mr. Walker. Yes. And then pumped it up to the treatment works. **Mr. Chester.** Why did they not keep it out?

Mr. Walker. They apparently prefer to handle such matters at the more remote treatment works, rather than in the city limits.

Mr. Chester. Instead of grinding it up and putting it back in, could they not have cremated it right there?

Mr. Walker. This, of course, could have been done, but the pumping station is rather old, built in 1898, and I saw an incinerator or other screenings disposal facilities. They are evidently of the opinion that the bulk of ground up screenings can be well handled and with the least offenses, in the sedimentation and sludge digestion tanks .

Mr. Chester. Your description of Moscow is good. It would fit some of the Japanese largest cities. They are well equipped with waterworks, but if you go into the interior country, in Japan, the situation is entirely different. You will find in their larger Japanese cities the same facilities, the same engineering priorities, as you saw in Moscow. But the situation in the country, as I say, is entirely different. May that be **U.S.S.R.** the situation in Russia?

Mr. Walker. Outside of the city?

Mr. Chester. Outside of the city. Cities of ten thousand population, we will say.

Mr. Walker. I made no personal inspections of the waterworks in any of the outside towns or small centers of population. On my visits to the Volga and the Oka Rivers and the various impounding reservoir sites, I traveled probably a thousand miles in the country around Moscow. On these excursions I passed through many towns and villages and I noted quite a few elevated tanks and water towers. One elevated tank was of interesting construction, with the supporting steel framework of small section spiral members, similar to the construction of the high lookout masts on battleships. This was designed by the Moscow Water Department. All of the waterworks in the towns and cities in the Province of Moscow, which takes in a territory within a radius of possibly 75 miles about the city, was charged to the Moscow Water Supply Board. I understand they have built new water supplies in 15 or 20 towns during the past few years. I believe, however, that in most of these small towns very few of the houses are pipes, and water is generally taken from street hydrants.

Mr. Chester. In talking with you I received some knowledge of the compensation received by the engineers and workers in Russia, which to me is extremely interesting. Would you give some of this information to the audience?

Mr. Walker. I heard so many conflicting reports concerning wages and salaries, that it is difficult to reduce them to average terms for the entire country. Ordinary labor, I understand, is paid anywhere from 2 or 3 up to 10 or 12 rubles a day. A ruble is equivalent to 51 1/2 cents. The rates vary to some extent upon the conditions, number of dependents, etc. The rates paid in Moscow are probably higher than in the rural districts. Many workers are paid on the piece work basis, including laborers on construction work. I have read that the average compensation to workers, for the entire country, is in the neighborhood of $50 to $60 per month.

Mr. Ledoux. American money?

Mr. Walker. Yes, this would be equivalent to 100 to 120 rubles.

Mr. Ledoux. Are they all paid in cash or in kind?

Mr. Walker. They are paid in cash, in rubles. Roughly, if our own cents, dollars and eagles were divided by two, it would be equivalent to the Russian kopeck, rubles and chervonetz. One chernonetz equals 10 rubles of 100 kopeck each.

Mr. Ledoux. How about the cost of living?

Mr. Walker. The cost of living is very high. The prices of food and clothing, on the average, are far higher than our prices. I am referring to the prices on the open markets. Workers have the benefit of special prices for many necessities and some luxuries, such as the opera, theaters, etc., but I must say it is difficult to understand how the people get along on $50 and $60 a month, with the cost of living as it is.

Mr. Chester. Does the peasant farmer pay his farmhand at that rate of compensation, including money and board?

Mr. Walker. I cannot answer that, Mr. Chester. I do not know how private help is paid. On the collective farms, I presume all help is paid by the government. Education of the peasants to go along on the collective farm basis, is probably one of the big problems. The government is spending millions of dollars on agriculture machinery, including giant combines, multiple ploughs, tractors, etc. I understand they are turning out tractors in large numbers, from their own plants. They are educating the peasants, furnishing them so I believe, with tractors and modern farm machinery to replace the old wooden ploughs, and instructing them in methods of scientific cultivation, so as to produce 10 bushels compared to one, with their old methods of three or four centuries ago.

Mr. Ledoux. Did you see very many beggars there?

Mr. Walker. Comparatively few. There were a few on the streets, peddling wares, but I did not see as many as on the streets here. Probably the reason is that their deserving poor, who are unable to work, are pretty well taken care of under their plan of social government.

They are doing some very remarkable things, some which compel attention and consideration, particularly in times like the present, with so many unemployed in our own country. I do not wish it be inferred that I am a convert to Communism, or that I am altogether in sympathy with everything they do, but I do say this: we should play fair with Russia. Since my visit there, I read everything I see dealing with the Russian situation, and with one exception, I have yet to see any articles in the public press which presented anything except the sore spots, and the darkest side of every subject, or gave any commendation or encouragement for the things they are doing or trying to do. We have a few sore spots here, and if newspaper men from Russia presented only to their readers a word picture of our present unemployment bread lines, soup kitchens, slums, bootlegging, racketeering, graft and political corruption to reduce them to average terms for the entire country, in general. And, I think we would be sore at them for not mentioning the many good things offsetting the ulcers and corruption which we deplore.

One of the things which impressed me is the support of the government in putting through the great five year plan, to the extent that the people are apparent willing to forgo present comforts and luxuries in border to attain the goal set by the program. I suppose most of you are familiar win a general way, with this plan, which every economist in the world is studying today. As I understand it, it is the most colossal scheme of coordination and budgeting ever undertaken by any government in the history of the world. It provides not only for the rational development of all threat natural resources of the country, but also includes all other activities of life such as transportation, education, culture, social services, public health and welfare, agriculture, home building, etc.

The present government inherited some territory problems. Following the war and revolution, it must have been a land of chaos. Crop failures and famine followed. All this is a vast country, three times as large as our own, with thousands of miles of their railroads destroyed during the war, and with only one out of every five literate. Now with conditions such as this, and handicapped by lack of credit, they get all together and develop this plan, and propose, by concentrated energy, entailing many sacrifices, to put the country on it's feet in five years' time and accomplish in that short period what it has taken other countries a couple of centuries to do. Everything is budgeted according to a prearranged schedule, and every phase of all activities must show progress from month to month. The plan is now two years old and I understand is actually ahead of schedule. The accomplishments already border on the miraculous. Surely with the great historical background of our own country, with it's beginning in a revolution to escape unjust persecutions and restrictions of personal liberties, we can, it would seem, extend our moral support at least to a people similarly endeavoring to work out of the chaos following an overthrow of autocracy and persecution.

Despite All the dire forebodings and forecasts of the failure and downfall of the present government, there is no evidence of it appearing on the surface in Moscow. Everybody is working and apparently full of pep and enthusiasm. There great trouble is scarcity of labor. Living conditions in overcrowded Moscow is not good, measured by our own standard, and many foodstuffs and comforts which we enjoy are not available at present. The transportation system is seriously overtaxed to handle the great volume of traffic incidental to the construction program, as well as the foodstuffs and other business. But despite of all the rumors of starvation bread and a few staples are plentiful, and they are certainly the healthiest look of healthiest people I ever saw.

But the people in general, are apparently willing to put up with these conditions temporarily, in the belief that all these things will be rectified when the great intensive work of reconstruction is completed in 1933, to be followed by a more leisurely development.

One of the things that commands attention is the social insurance scheme. Practically all business, as you probably know, is government operated. This includes factories, public utilities, stores, hotels, theaters, taxicabs, etc. The people are paid by the government and in turn buy all their needs, and pay rent to the government for their homes.

While the wages are low and limited in amount, so that no one can get rich, workers enjoy certain benefits under the social insurance plan, which insures, to some extent, freedom from the fears of poverty and distress. There are many benefits under this scheme. They are taken care of in old age and sickness.

Mr. Ledoux. What age?

Mr. Walker. I don't know of any fixed age limit but if unable to work, they are taken care o0f. If out of employment they receive a dole of one fifth of their wages, for a period of from six to nine months.

One of the most remarkable things is what this system has done for the women, who, under the Tsars Regime, had no liberties, and were practically beasts of burden. The new government places women on equality with men in every respect. In my humble opinion, if this government succeeds, the women are going to have a large share of the credit. They are eligible for all work and activities, from common laborers and street cleaners, to the highest governmental, professional and technical positions. It is quite startling to see them digging ditches or working on section gangs on the railroads.

On my first visit to one of the filter plants, I received sort of a jolt when I was inspecting some new construction work. I have always assumed that field engineers work was primarily a man's job, but here I saw two groups of girls engaged with transit, level rod and chain laying out forms for new filters. I said to Serge, my interpreter, "Are they school girls, learning something about surveying?" He said, "No, they are our engineer corp." (Laughter)

Engineers are scarce in Russia. And I was informed they are training thousands of young girls in engineering and related lines. During my seven weeks in Moscow, I did a lot of trolley car riding (trams they call them), and I personally observed five or six girls, on different occasions, studying engineer subjects on their way to work.

61

I got a little off my subject, and meant to tell you more about the social insurance benefits. As I understand it, in cases of death in a family, a bonus of one month's wages is paid to cover funeral expenses. Cremation is general in these cities.

When a child is born, the parents receive an increase of 25% in wages to pay for the child's support, up to the age of 16 years.

Full wages are paid during illness, and all medical attention, drugs, and hospital care are free, the doctors being paid by the government.

Under present conditions, women, single and married, work the same as men, in all lines. If there are children, the older ones get their breakfast and lunch in the schools, and the parents in the factory kitchens. Nurseries and kindergartens are provided in the factories for the young children, under the care of nurses and teachers.

Great care is taken of expectant mothers. As soon as she knows she is to become a mother, she is required to report to the hospital at least once a month for the first seven months, where she is under supervision and is given advice on prenatal care. She then goes on vacation, with full pay, for three to four months (four if she is a physical worker), but is required to report to the hospital every week, until the birth, for examination and to draw her pay. All children are born in the hospital. When the child is two months old the mother may resume her work, consigning the child to the care of the nursery during the working hours, with time off during intervals to nurse it. I was informed that almost all Russian women nurse their babies, and that the bottle babies are comparatively few. I think you will agree that many of these things are rather remarkable.

You hear a great deal of criticism as to the morals of the country and the divorce question. As far as I could see the morals of Moscow were superior to most other large cities. There is practically no night life as we term it. There is no such thing s naturalization of women. As to marriage and divorce, they have been reduced to nothing more than a matter of registration. But as I understand it, the system was not arbitrarily forced on the people, but was the result of an extended study and questionnaire sent throughout the country. Under the old marriage laws, women were chattels, they had no rights whatever. Now they have equal rights with men, in every particular.

It is true that divorce is a very simple matter, where there are no children, and it is not contested. The government simply takes the stand that if a husband and wife cannot get along together, and mutually agree to separate, that it is a personal matter, and the state will not compel them to live together out of harmony. But if there are children, it is not so easy, and it is referred to a board of hearing. In such cases divorce is granted only after provision is made for support of the child until it is 16 years old. It is an interesting matter for speculation, in connection with divorce in Russia, that lawyers do not appear anywhere in the picture.

Marriage or divorce do not cost the contracting parties a kopeck. In America, so I am told, there are 17 divorces out of every 100 marriages, which provides quite a bit of business for our lawyer friends. They couldn't make much of a living from this business in Russia. (Laughter) In fact, I am afraid Russia would not be a lucrative field for the legal fraternity as the entire legal structure is cleared of it's mystic muse and greatly simplified laws mean what they say and are enforced without ceremony. The people there simply cannot understand our situation with regard to gangsters, gunmen, and racketeering. Gentlemen of this caliber in Russia, would be out of the picture in 24 hours time.

Mr. Chester. What is the percentage of divorces there?

Mr. Walker. I did not obtain those figures. I doubt if it is as high as our own.

Mr. Chester. How do people in our business live, do they live in a few rooms, or get a small salary?

Mr. Walker. The lack of proper housing is so serious vat present, that there is much overcrowding. I understand that many of the larger houses of say 12 or 15 rooms, are now accommodating six or eight families. Very comfortable apartment houses are being constructed for the workers, each apartment consisting of two large rooms, a kitchen and a bath. I lived in one of these myself, during the last month of my stay.

I did not visit any of the engineers in their homes, but presume they live in quarters similar to the rest of the people. As to salary, they are limited in amount, the same as the other workers. But they are paid higher than any other profession.

Mr. Ledoux. Do the higher officials live in the same way?

Mr. Walker. I understand, since the revolution, the highest officials live in the palaces in the Kremlin. I presume, however, that this will be changed upon completion of the great new government building. I believe it is the intention to throw open the Kremlin to tourists when the government offices are removed. I have been frequently asked if the head officials are not getting rich at the expense of the people. There is certainly no evidence of it. As I understand it, communist officials are limited in salary to a maximum of about $115 to $125 dollars a month. Grafting is a pretty dangerous proceeding. I was told that if any one was caught at it, they are lined up against a brick wall and shot.

Mr. Chester. Do they still have an aristocracy?

Mr. Walker. No.

Mr. Walker. When I say aristocracy, I mean, for instance a man getting one thousand dollars a month or some larger salary. As I said, engineers are paid higher than any other profession. It is one country where they think we are worthy of some consideration. I was told that some of the outstanding engineers are paid up to 1,000 rubles, or $500 dollars a month.

Mr. Carmack. It is not possible, is it for them to abolish distinction between men?

Mr. Walker. No, not in that sense.

Mr. Carmack. They give us the impression that they are always endeavoring to reduce the entire population to a common level, the level of proletarian. I was wondering how they would be able to progress on that scheme, and develop good men for leadership. I did not see how it would be possible for them to reduce the men to a common level, as they appear to be trying to do and still have all this technical knowledge, and these wonderful improvements which you have spoken of.

Mr. Walker. I don't know if I fully understand your question, Mr. Carmack.

Mr. Carmack. It is almost impossible, it seems to me, to put an entire population upon a common level.

Mr. Walker. Possibly I do not get by your idea as to common level. I have referred to the remuneration of the lowest laborers up to the highest paid engineers. There is no such thing as an aristocracy or wealthy class.

Mr. Carmack. Well, I suppose I illustrated by saying that they are trying to put the peasant on the same level as the intellectual man.

Mr. Walker. If you mean by common level that everybody is on the same level intellectually why of course that is impossible. All people have not the same brain capacity, or capacity for acquiring knowledge, so from that standpoint, while government can give the ignorant as well as the intelligent, equal rights and liberties under the law, they cannot establish equality as to intelligence, breeding and inherent refinements. In order to raise the standard of intelligence among the people, however, they are spending millions upon their educational system. This is all a part of the five year plan.

As I understand it, under the Tsar, only about one out of every five people were literate. This was due to the large peasant population being kept submerged in ignorance. This type, however, is not unknown outside of Russia. We have in some of our own remote mountain sections people who, as to educational accomplishments, are on a par with the Russian peasant. It is to correct these condition, that the government is compelling illiterate adults to attend school, and learn to read and write, and are also using other means such as the radio, newspapers, and other literature, traveling libraries, communist clubs and also, so called Red Corners, to reach the maximum number of people in the shortest time. I have been informed that they have already increased the percentage of literates from about 22% to 55 or 60%, and claims that by 1933, the termination of the five year plan, all persons in the country between the ages of eight and 40 years will be able to read and write.

Mr. Carmack. I was wondering how these highly skilled technical men and engineers would be willing to live on these small salaries and under the conditions there.

Mr. Walker. The only way I can answer that is to say that none of the engineers with whom I came in contact with, seemed noticeably depressed. They were regular fellows, good company, liked a good joke or story, enjoyed a cigar or cigarette, or a glass of wine or vodka, and were really interested in their work, also in the arts, music and world events.

Mr. Ledoux. How do they care for children, for instance, of a woman who is not married?

Mr. Walker. Well, I believe they take the stand that if a child is born, it must have a father.

Mr. Ledoux. Yes, if they can find him.

Mr. Walker. I understand that in most cases they do find him. At least if responsibility cannot be definitely established, but promiscuous relations are shown with different men, some one or possibly all found implicated, are held liable for the support of the child.

Mr. Ledoux. Does the woman have to support the child, or how is the child supported in the event a father is not found?

Mr. Walker. I am afraid I am jot versed in all those details, Mr. Ledoux. I presume, in that case, the child is cared for in a government institution, as all destitute children under 16 years, are provided for under the social insurance plan. Under their system there is no stigma on a child born out of wedlock.

One thing of interest, in connection with their divorce laws, which I don't believe I mentioned, is that under certain conditions, with women and men being on equal footing, she may be required to pay alimony to the husband, in case of a contested divorce, where she is in the wrong.

The President. That is, if the man is unable and the woman is able?

Mr. Walker. Yes. (Laughter)

The President. Mr. Walker is going to be around for awhile, and you will have the opportunity to ask him questions.

Mr. Ledoux. I think his paper is the most illuminating one that has been read for quite some time. If he had been employed for that purpose, I do not think it could have been ,more skillfully prepared. (Laughter) I think he deserves the greatest credit in the world. (Applause)

Mr. Carmack. I was wondering about a remark that Mr. Walker made as to the attitude of the press. I think the papers in this country have not been fair to Russia. They have not given us real information from the people who know. I do not think it is right.

The President. I think we are fortunate in having Mr. Walker with us this afternoon. He has given us a most interesting paper, certainly very illuminating, as Mr. Ledoux said. Mr. Walker is going to be here until about 3.00 o'clock this afternoon. I have no doubt he would like to stay up here on the platform and talk to you for a considerable length of time, because he has an interesting subject, and a wide knowledge of it, and evidently from the responses here, one of great interest. He told me before he came that he would be glad to talk informally to anybody, or to some of you men in groups, outside. I do not think that we ought to take any more time this afternoon with discussion of this paper, much as we have enjoyed it, because we have others on the program. So, we will now take up the last paper on the program for this afternoon, which is the third on the printed program, "Economics of Rate Making." by Nicholas S. Hill, Jr., of New York. This paper also will be read by Mr. Siems.

1930 USSR Trip

Isaac Stanley Walker's Personal Photo Album

Moscow, from Voriobsky Reservoir. June 6th, 1930

Oldenborg Pumping Station. June 5th

Volga River near Gorodisha. Peasants Wagons. June 20th

Rubleva Pumping Station, New Building. June 4th

Inlet and Gate Chambers
Variobesky Reservoir.
June 6th

Volga River near Gorodisha
Mr. Goshin. F.S.Walker. J. Skinner.
Chief Engr.   Commissar Kanyguine
Water Works.   June 20th

Luncheon at Oka River
Experimental Station.
June 9th

Rubleva Pumping Station
Old Building
June 4th

Rubleva Pumping Station Interiors
June 4th

Meter Shop. Oldenborg.
June 5th

Pipe Yard. Oldenborg
June 5th

Moscow River. Half-dams
opposite Rubleva Intake.
June 4th

Moscow River.- Downstream
from Rubleva Intake.

Moscow River. Upstream
from Rubleva Intake.

Cake Alum used in filtration.
J.F.Skinner & Supt. Rubleva Filter Plant
June 4th

New Pre-filters. Rubleva.   June 4th

New Mixing Basin & Pre-filter

Coffer Dam for Moscow River   Moscow River. Coffer dam from
June 6th   the Coffer dam Bridge

On trip to Oka River
June 9th

Laboratory Building
Oka River Experimental Station
June 9th

On trip to Estra-River
Center Mr. Kondrashov, Project Engr.
June 7th

Peasant's wagon upset
Volga River near Gorodisha.
June 20th

View of Oka River above Experimental Station, and proposed future Pumping Station
June 9th

Luncheon on trip to Volga River
June 20th

Estra River Dam Site
June 7th

Pasture. Area will be Flooded
by Estra Impounding Reservoir.

Village near Estra Dam Site
Voskresensk

Peasant's Home. Voskresensk

Roof of Vorobesty Covered Reservoir
June 6th

Roof of Flow Sand Filters at Rublevo
June 4th

Volga River at Kosino

Trostensky Lake. Ozerna Reserve
June 7th

Peasant's Home
on trip to Estra River.
June 7th

E-3-41

Caravan of Peasants wagons
Near Volga River
June 20th

E-3-42

J.F. Skinner

E-3-43

Close view of Peasant's Log House
on trip to Estra River.

Righting Peasant Wagon upturned
after horse became frightened at
approach of auto. Near Volga River

E-3-44

Main Sewage Pumping Station
June 1st

E-3-47

Serge (Interpreter)   S.A.A. Foto (Ass't Engr)
Professor S.N. Stroganoff (Chemist &
                          Bacteriologist)
June 1st

E-3-48

Hospital for Workers, Lubertzy.
June 1st

E-3-49

E-3-50

Collecting Ravine - Lubertzy Fields
Note bank protection.
June 1st

Constructing new sand beds, Lubertzy.
Hand labor.

Low Fields - Pipeline.
June 2nd

Distributing Channel to low fields.

Main Feed Conduit at Lubertzy
Filtration Fields.

Main Feed Conduit, Lubertzy.

Conduit Junction.

Trash Rack in Conduit.

EXPERIMENTAL STATION AT LUBLINO

Contact Beds

Trickling Filters

Aerating Trickling Filter

Traveling Distributor, Trickling Filter

KOGUHOVSKY ACTIVATED SLUDGE PLANT

Aerating Trickling Filters

Aerating Trickling Filters

Artificial Stone Tanks

Sedimentation Tanks

KOGUHOVSKY ACTIVATED SLUDGE PLANT

Sedimentation Tanks

Fish Pond for Sewage Effluent

Plant Extensions under Construction

Serac, J.S.W.

Drive, Rublevo Pumping Station

Corner Tower
Simonosky Monastery
O.C. 14th Century for 1st
Photo taken 4 AM from
5th Floor of Sarabrick Apart-
ments, opposite
Moscow

Russian Peasant Children

J.F. Skinner. — Caretaker.
Monument.

Museum

At Borodino Battlefield, near Ruza, U.S.S.R.
Napoleon's Invasion of Russia, in 1812.

Russian Forest
White Birches.

Peasants' Homes
Russia.

Street - View from 5th floor
Seabrook Apartment Building

Herd of Cows
Russia.

Peasants' Wagon fording Stream
Russia.

Jerusalem Church,
Built 1656. Voiskresensk Village,
on trip to Estra River

Stolpce Station, Poland.
May 30.

Communist Workers Club,
near Lublertzy Sewage Fields

R.R. Station, Poland.
May 30.

Engine - Polish R.R.
May 30

Niegoroje Station - Russian Border
Legend on Arch over tracks reads
"Communism erases all Boundary Lines."
May 30.

J.F. Skinner.   A.H. Hoski.
Brief Stop in Poland.
May 30

Gardens - Potsdam.
May 29.

Unter-den-Linden, Berlin.
May 28.

Unter-den-Linden, Berlin
May 28

L.S.W.   R.F.Bessey
Sans Souci, Potsdam.
May 29

Unter den Linden, Berlin.
May 28.

Roy F. Bessey   Pilsener   German Guide   Munchner   Wurzburner
Stop en route to Potsdam.
May 29

Palace Grounds Potsdam
May 29

Old Mill, Potsdam
May 29

Cold Bath
Vast Adornment Grounds
May 29.

J.F. Skinner
Mrs. Stephenson
Coston Stephenson

At Windsor Castle, England
July 13

I.S. Walker
Mrs. Stephenson

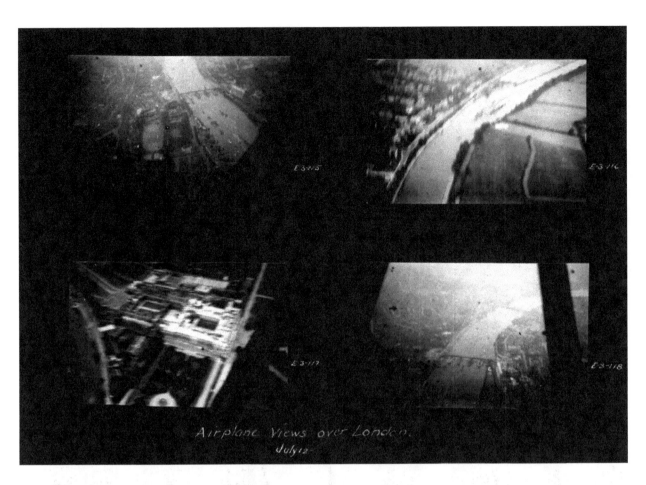

Airplane Views over London.
July 12.

Capt & Mrs. Stephenson.
Surrey, England
July 13

Miss Gleason, from
July 18.

Battlefield, Berzy le sec France.
Mr. Skinner
Note Cave bomb-proof. Remnants of the Big Drive.
July 18

Shrapnel Marks - Soissons Cathedral, France.
July 18

Interior - Soissons Cathedral.
July 18.

View in Cherbourg, France
July 18

Sld ruins of Castle 6th Century.

J.F.Skinner

Views from Turret of La Tour Carrée (Miss Gleasons Chateau) Berzy le Sec, France
July 18.

Sun Deck
S.S. Bremen
May 24.

Boat Deck S.S. Bremen
May 24

Sun Deck S.S. Bremen
May 24.

S.S. Bremen
May 24

S.S. Bremen
May 24.

Deck Sports S.S. Bremen
May 24

Boats Cherbourg Harbor

E 3-155

S.S. Bremen
"Grosspacks", ready for landing

E 3-156

E 3-157

Bremerhaven Wharf

E 3-158

E 3-159

E 3-160

E 3-161

S.S. New York, approaching
Cherbourg, France

E 3-162

ISW with a Russian cow!

Russian Postcards from ISW's Collection

St. Basil Cathedral.

Kremlin.

Moscow River.

Typical Street scene. - Moscow.

Academy of the Red Army.

Great Academic State Theatre.
Opera and Ballet.

Kremlin.

Alexander Gardens.

Briansky R.R. Station.

Sources

Holliday, George, D., *Technology Transfer to the USSR, 1928-1937 and 1966-1975: The Role of Western Technology in Soviet Economic Development*, Westview Press, Boulder Colorado, 1979.

Siegel, Katherine, A.S., *Loans and Legitimacy: The Evolution of Soviet-American Relations 1919-1933*, University of Kentucky, The University of Kentucky Press, 1966.

An American Engineer in Stalin's Russia: The Memoirs of Zara Witkin 1932-1934, Edited with an Introduction
by Michael Gelp, University of California Press, 1991.

Sutton, Anthony C., *Western Technology and Soviet Economic Development 1930 to 1945*, Hoover Institution,
Stanford University, 1971.

Over the Spillway - Life Journey of an Engineers, Compiled and Edited by William Alan Walker, Jr. and Joan Walker Miskell, WalkerMiskell Publishing, 2015.